IF THE EYE BE SOUND...

★

Thomas Cullinan

IF THE EYE
BE SOUND...

 St Paul Publications

ST PAUL PUBLICATIONS
SLOUGH SL3 6BT ENGLAND

Copyright © St Paul Publications 1975
Nihil obstat: G.E. Roberts
Imprimatur: + Charles Grant, Bishop of Northampton
              8 October 1975
First published December 1975
Printed in Great Britain by the Society of St Paul, Slough
SBN 85439 120 7

CONTENTS

Acknowledgements

Extracts from Edwin Muir 'The Refugees' from his *Selected Poems;* and T.S. Eliot's 'The Rock' from *Collected Poems, 1909-62.* Copyright by Faber & Faber Ltd.

Psalms are in the Grail version.

Thomas Merton, chapter XVII of *The Climate of Monastic Prayer.* Copyright by Cistercian Publications, Spencer, Mass.

FOREWORD

Dear Reader,

Whatever you find of value in these pages comes to you from the confluence of two streams which you may think have little in common. One is the monastic tradition which has formed my life for twenty years; the other is the work of the Commission for International Justice and Peace * over the last four.

It is to the members of the latter that the book should be dedicated. It has been their stimulus which has challenged my own understanding of the world we live in and it is at their request that this rag-bag of talks and papers is published for you.

We have tried to remove the inevitable repetitions in a collection from so varied origins. But in order to preserve the original character of the talks, there are still repetitions asking for your forgiveness.

One of those who read the typescript complained that I have not offered clear solutions. Let me explain:

---

* Commission of the Catholic Bishops of England & Wales.

In science and technology we can produce and work from blueprints for the future. In human affairs there are none. It is easier to go to the moon than build homes for people.

At a moment in history when we are threatened by social forces apparently beyond our control men feel lost in a wilderness or trapped in a prison. But events or situations are never themselves trapping, it is only our limited and conditioned interpretation of them. There is an alternative to fear and dissolution, the art of bringing new light to bear. When expectations dwindle, hope arises, not from a new set of blueprints about how to deliver the goods, but from bringing fresh criteria to our assessment.

If the eye be sound the whole body will be light — and the eye can only become sound by means of an inner awakening and *metanoia* beyond what our immediate conditioning can supply.

Shalom,

Thomas Cullinan

Ampleforth Abbey
August 1975

FEEDING THE HUNGRY OR
FEEDING THE BEAST?

(To Oxfam organisers, March 1974)

A Parable: One day, over a decade ago, Sebastian first experienced a dread in his guts that behind the statistics and behind the news items and behind the successive famine emergencies lay a fundamental truth about himself and his world which he could no longer ignore. In fact it was a double dread: what would his own life mean if he did not link it with those who live and die in hunger? and what would happen to a world which refused to serve first those in greatest need?

So, in 1960 he found Oxfam, then a one-horse *charity* in a few rooms in Queen Street, trying to get, and send on, food, clothing and money.

In 1963 he began to see that giving people things was only a stop gap answer. Indeed, in some ways it made things worse. What was needed was concern for *development,* to help people to feed themselves; not food, clothing and money, but fertilisers, tools and schools.

In 1966 he was quite shaken when he realized that the people who harvested the coffee he drank every day lived at starvation level, and the man who mined the tin in which the coffee came, earned £7 a month in a Bolivian tin mine and warded off hunger by chewing coca leaves. Sebastian stopped talking about charity and started talking about *justice*.

In 1969 he came to see that the injustice done against so many destitute people was not just a simple injustice between groups of people in the world. He came to see it as *structural injustice*. That it is the very economic and social structures that we operate which work profound injustice against the destitute and that we are all involved in such structures, whether Sebastian likes it or not.

In 1972, Sebastian moved to a further level of response. He began to see that what was really at stake was not people's hunger for more money, food or health, but their hunger for life, for freedom and culture. He saw that the profoundest form of underdevelopment and of oppression is the moral state of men who have sapped out of them any desire to shape their own history. They have no inner ability to call life their own, they have been treated for so long as the object of other men's decisions, that they have lost the spiritual ability to say 'I matter, I will stand up and shape things'.

He saw that this was the ultimate injustice of men against men, and could only be met by what the Latin American thinkers and theologians mean by *liberation*. He found this a big shift on from his previous thinking.

In 1974, Sebastian came to see that he, Sebastian, was very much a child of his own time. That whatever he might give of his money or his time or his understanding, the place where his first and fundamental response must be, was *within himself*.

10

Such progressive stages in awareness are known not only to many individuals beside Sebastian but are also *roughly* the way that thinking has progressed among voluntary agencies and others during the last decade or so. It is not that each stage invalidates the previous one, any more than a need for social medicine invalidates the ambulance service; but each stage does demand a new response at a deeper level.

We notice first about these stages, that what starts as a problem about them over there, overseas, increasingly becomes a problem about us. We can say in a far wider international sense what Cosmos Desmond said of the limited South African context: It is enough that they show us what we have made of them for us to realize what we have made of ourselves. We notice also, that what starts as an external concern on the periphery of one's life becomes interiorized, affecting and calling on our life at its very centre. We will perhaps notice too, that what starts as a desire to help people, as it were from without, turns into a desire to identify with them in suffering, to share in a way that costs oneself and not merely to help in a way that calms one's conscience. The other week I was in the office of the Catholic Housing Aid Society. They had just received two letters, one beautifully typed and headed and offering sympathy for the work, signed Sir so-and-so. The other, a scruffy little note apologizing for so small a contribution, merely signed 'OAP in Hull'. Each enclosed £1. But the first was almost an insult of condescension and the latter a truly sacramental gift of self. We all know that giving to charity *must* grow into a yearning to identify and to share, but alas our armchairs are so comfy.

We notice too, in this progress of understanding, a

11

shift away from solutions merely in terms of food and fertilizer, of health and housing. All these are of course, important, but only as a means to a far deeper cultural reality: the growth of a local or national culture with which people can truly identify, in which, that is, they have a sense of belonging, in which they have to make decisions and to be responsible for their own history, their own culture. In Belfast or Derry, what is more sad than all the violence in this cultural collapse and the deep moral apathy of people who have no response in themselves other than to wait for someone else to solve their problems and bring solutions.

It was encouraging last summer to find, in Ballymurphy, catalysts at work who have encouraged them not to wait for schools, but to start their own, and start their own factory, run their own summer festival of acting, music and poetry all from local talent previously hidden in secret, behind doors. And it is basically the same approach one meets with the Bogside Community Association, in Derry. Those in Oxfam know of dozens of cases, all over the world, where westerners and perhaps missionaries as much as any, have had to learn with great pain that it is more important for people to stand on their own feet, be able to call life *their* life and culture *their* culture, than it is to have what we would call a standard of living. Man's hunger for bread is only an expression and a symptom of his hunger for life. It's only a measure of our own western materialism that we so often fail to see this.

When we Catholics had a large Eucharistic Congress in Bombay a few years ago, word went out to keep it very simple, India is a starving nation. But an Indian priest replied, when he saw the stark simplicity of what had been provided: 'Woe to you, you western materialists, you feed too well and then cut down on your worship and celebration of God. We in India would rather go without supper tonight in order to pay for a festival for God tomorrow'.

Lastly we notice in this progress of understanding, and perhaps most important of all, that Sebastian started by thinking that the poor overseas and the poor at home were largely accidental to our own social order, in the sense that were they not there we could get on O.K., or in the sense that, given time, everyone will climb on the bandwagon and then everyone will be O.K. But he now sees, on the contrary, that it is the very same processes in our social order which feed the fed up as deny life to the destitute; that the rich need the poverty of the poor more than the poor need the riches of the rich. This is a very painful moment of awareness.

Painful because it shatters many of our illusions and makes many demands on us which we would rather not face. It's the very simple truth that our cultural story is written, the main text of our cultural story, precisely for those who are already there and that the processes by which we do this thrust into the margin as embarrassments millions of people in the Third World and indeed within the pockets of urban poverty at home, those who can't make it. Our captitalist growth economy of its very nature, titivates and excites and encourages those already in its main text, and by that very process casts into the margins the inadequate, the dispossessed, the uprooted. This specialization of power, of decision-making, of technology, is an integral part of our political and social reality today. It is important, I think, that we feel within ourselves,

13

within our thinking, within our interpretation of what happens, that it really is the same processes that set up some of us as destroy others.

Now when Sebastian had found himself dragged through these stages of awareness he began to feel a great sense of impotence, of inability to move forward. He began to experience that profound sense of being caught up in the dominion of the beast which lays claim to the lives not only of those in the margins, but also those in the main text. This is the very widespread feeling of despair and alienation that we experience today. People cry out, as in John's dream, 'who can free us from the beast?' at the same time as giving themselves over to it and to its ideology. For the beast claims total dominion over the lives of men. It causes all 'both small and great, both rich and poor, both free men and slaves to be marked on the right hand or the forehead so that no-one can buy or sell unless he has the mark'.

It is the absolute totalitarian claim of the dominion of the beast set by St John * over against the dominion and the sovereignty of God. Sebastian was experiencing what it is to be caught up in a colossal system which dominates the commerce, the lives, and the decisions of men, but which seems to be beyond their control to change. He felt that perhaps all the work he did at Oxfam was merely playing about in front of the political and economic structures which in fact destroy the lives of people. He had that sense of dread that maybe his work, for all its generosity and good will, might even be feeding the beast because it gave the appearance of answering basic needs

---

* Revelation, chapter 13.

while in fact not touching the root causes. He now knew what people meant by the innate violence of modern society and he came to see that this unrecognized violence was far more serious than the overt violence about which people get so alarmed. But what could he do? Certainly, the greatest victory which the beast can have is to build up in people a sense of complete alienation and impotence. The despair of being able to do absolutely nothing about it. Perhaps he should join those who dream up complete alternative blueprints, as if the only answer was to start all over again, with a non-capitalist, non-growth economy, non-acquisitive society. But that too could be merely play-boy dreaming, lacking political realism in the here and the now. No, he had to persuade himself of the infinite capacity of the human spirit to transcend any system and structure, while living within it and this must mean one thing to start with — self knowledge.

Now Sebastian was of middle-class rather bourgeois background, and it was only gradually that he discovered in himself how many inherited illusions and myths he had received. For instance, there was the trickle-through-myth. That is, if those who are pampered in the main text of society, the rich nations internationally, the well-off middle class or organized working class in our country, if these are pampered and encouraged enough, then sooner or later it is bound to flow through to the margins. But he discovered that all the economic evidence is in fact against this; that if anything, the gap between the main text and the margin tends to become wider. Then there was the poor-are-always-with-you myth. But as we have seen he already knew that poverty doesn't just happen but is caused, and that he was involved in those causes. Then there was the no-poverty-only-bad-management myth. That beautifully simple expression of the Protestant ethic which allows the successful to look with some disdain on those who are not. Sebastian found that this inherited myth connected with all sorts of other matters. For instance, it took a very long time for him to stop thinking that the different incomes enjoyed by different people or indeed the different wealth of different nations, were a measure of the work they did or of their value to people, and to start really to grasp that these differences of income are really a measure of various values and systems of society at large. He was alarmed to discover how he had mentally assumed that a high standard of living is a measure of personal hard work and high standard of management. And this brought him on to a myth, an illusion, which he suspected lay at the heart of much of his basic inter-pretation of life. It was the What's-mine-is-mine-isn't-it? myth. He found in himself two conflicting interpretations of what it meant to *own* something, to have something at his disposal.

One was the white, Anglo-Saxon Protestant approach, which he presumed was in him as a result of the social, religious, political thinking of the last few hundred years of Western history. This made him feel that what was his was his, and that if he chose to use it or store it away in a bank that was O.K.; if he chose to give some to people in need that was generosity on his part and certainly deserved gratitude from the recipients. But there was another approach also, which he found expressed clearly in the Old Testament and in a new way in the teachings of Christ and indeed in much of Christian thinking and history. It was this, that everything in his life is a *gift*: his time, his abilities, his interests, his money, gift mediated through his own family background, his education, the social structure he found himself in, but nonetheless gift. He came to see that gifts are always for sharing.

To put it another way; private ownership always presupposes a communal reference. This proved to be a terrific shift in his interpretation of life, especially as many of his friends seemed to have a deep guilt feeling about being middle-class, and white, and first worldly. But such guilt is death-dealing and Sebastian felt that creativity and life would come not from guilt but from gratitude. Because gratitude and joy are truer motivations for sharing and identifying with the destitute than is guilt. Things and time, ability and the power to make decisions, all are gifts, and gifts are essentially for opening life out and for making friends and for serving those in need, not for closing life in, for defending and protecting oneself. When Sebastian looked at our National Defence Budget he began to see the implications of having things to defend. But then locking his own front door was only part of the same thing.

Now such self-knowledge and the discoveries involved have no limits, but it is essential if a person or an organization is to become not merely a plaything of the beast but a creative self able to move forward to new things. It is always a painful process and it needs quite a discipline of mind because we do not see the reality of who we really are, of what it means to be me, to be us, unless we really decide to centre our attention on what matters. This question of self-knowledge is central to our situation today and I'd like to give you a parallel example from my own experience, because we can really only talk about ourselves.

17

What should I do in finding myself both a monk and a public school-teacher when I don't, as it happens, find the two fit together very easily? I could mud sling with antis, I suppose, or join the nervous defensiveness of the pros. But neither of these really open up the future.

So I think we start, in such situations (and most of us are involved in similar ones of one sort or another) by asking: 'Who are we?' Well we are white in a world that generally isn't. We are English or British, or whatever; we are middle-class; we are male in a world which is only half male. You don't start by feeling guilty about it and you don't start by feeling proud about it. You simply start by saying this is what we are and what does it mean to be these things? What does it mean to be middle-class today within the social whole that is our country and the social whole that is the world? If we can answer those questions we are in a position to move forward to new things. If we don't face those questions then all the rest of the discussion seems to me to be pointless because it's already working on lack of wisdom and lack of knowledge. But these questions are painful. It certainly means when we start that we don't have a clear blueprint of alternatives. People tend to say we can't be anything other than we are because we have no nice clear alternatives. I think this is nonsense. I think we start by saying 'let's see who we are', because in the answering of that question and really facing it we are led forward to new things, and the alternatives grow.

But the questions are painful and people know they are painful before they start asking them, and that's why it is much easier to bury our heads in the work we are doing. Also, I think the questions of self-knowledge are

18

bound to make demands on the way we live our life: what people nowadays call *lifestyle*. Questions of self-knowledge make demands on us that shift what we think is important and the way we use the things which we've always taken for granted. I'm going to come back to that later on in a slightly different context. Questions of self-knowledge are simple and naive when we first meet them; if we really ask them and face their consequences then they turn out to be painful and demanding, but extremely exciting and maybe the only thing really creative.

I would like now to make three points for everyone and then a footnote for Christians in particular.

First of all we have a tendency nowadays, because we are rather good at things and because we are able to achieve so much, to lose ourselves in the work we are doing, and to think that any worries and problems can be solved by doing more and more work, longer and longer hours and so on. I think this is fatal and unless we find in our lives — and make decisions so that we do find — an ability to withdraw in order to engage again at a deeper level, then the whole process of getting to know ourselves and what we can look forward to in the future cannot happen. We simply dissipate our energies all the time in the work we're doing. And in the long run and probably in the short run, we haven't got more to give than what is in us. If there is nothing inside us then all our activities are simply a blind, however good it looks and however much people think we're doing a wonderful job. I think this is a very important thing. If you want to follow up a superb discussion of it and you have access somewhere to Arnold Toynbee's great book on history, you will find he goes through this pattern of engaging in a social issue, then

19

learning to withdraw from it, to see the thing at a deeper level and as it really is and then re-engaging at a deeper level. He traces this pattern in the lives of many great men who have changed the history of the world. And really we have to go through this same process as individuals and organizations in some way. But withdrawing isn't always the same as endless talk; in fact we have to look quietly into ourselves as well. That's one point.

A second point is that we have somehow to be aware of the whole scene in which the world is and in which we are working and yet at the same time know that we have only a limited area in which we can operate. Some young people — one finds this at the top ends of schools and sometimes in universities — because there is so much information around and so much communication, tend to take on their shoulders the weight of all the world's problems and they get weighed down by it and wonder why they can do nothing about it. Well somehow, we have got to have a very wide vision of what history is and the context in which we're working, and yet know that we are limited people with a limited job to do and it's got to be done thoroughly. I've always appreciated this, if he won't mind my saying so, in Leslie Kirkley, because there have been many pressures on him to dissipate Oxfam's energies by taking up all sorts of further work. Somehow he's maintained a broad vision of the context in which we're all involved and yet has said: This is our job and this is our contribution, and I think the balance between those two is very powerful. I think it's probably what St Paul meant by administrators must be constant with their administration, teachers with their teaching, preachers with their preaching and not start taking on everyone else's job at the same time, because then you're quite certain not to do your own properly.

The third point which I think is enormously important, is that if we have a vision of society being free of various things that are present in it, then we must start within ourselves and within our own organization. We can't create a non-acquisitive society if our organization itself is acquisitive. We can't create a society which is free of a cult of success if our own organization is cultivating success. I think one little aspect of this is that we must be very, very careful not to be more interested in our organizations than in the people we are existing to serve. Sometimes even amongst voluntary agencies, one feels a certain competitive approach of one agency to another. Sometimes it slips out by mistake in the way we talk, betraying what might be going on at the back of our minds, that we're more interested in Oxfam than the people who are destitute and in need. This is very dangerous, because the organization becomes what we exist for and not the people, and in the end it's only people that matter. In general, in a wider way our organizations must prefigure that which we are trying to achieve in society. That was Gandhi's great insight. How wrong it is to think that we can set up any organization or means in order to achieve an end because it's the steps we take towards the end that create what we finish with. As Eldridge Cleaver said, criticizing James Baldwin for going white in his lifestyle, 'if you are not part of the solution then it must be that you are part of the problem itself'. I find that a very challenging thought.

And now my footnote for Christians: we must not under-estimate in the process of discovering in ourselves who we are, the extent to which our Western Christianity has formed the Gospel into a support operation for what we want to do anyhow. God originally makes man in his own image and likeness and then man spends most of his history forming God into the image that he wants him to be for his own purpose.

We were given a Gospel that was a wild tiger, we tame it and domesticate it into a pussycat. We have tried to say yes to God and yes to everything we want to do in our modern Western, Anglo-Saxon society at the same time. Anyone who knows the history of Christianity in this country and in the West will know what I mean.

A few weeks ago, before the election, we had a meeting in Warrington with our three prospective candidates. In a slightly scurrilous moment I decided to jot down some of the words which during the course of the evening people used to describe being 'Christian'. The first three I wrote down were compassion, conciliation and commonsense. People were saying to the candidates· 'why in our industrial relations can't we be more Christian? We must have compassion, conciliation and commonsense'. Well that is domesticating what we were given. It's making it into a nice-to-get-on-with-each-other politeness. It is saying 'if there's any trouble then it's not the Gospel' and 'as long as there's no trouble then it must be all right'. It's not what I find in the Gospel.

One aspect of this domesticating process is to use the Gospel as a technique for solving our problem, rather than as a response to the God-ness of God. An example: There is a movement started by some Christians called 'Lifestyle'. Lifestyle spells out various ways in which people can simplify the way they live, in order to be more ecologically and politically relevant. In order to make it attractive to non-Christians who do not share their beliefs, they have cut out of the preamble any reference to God or the Gospel. But if you read St Luke you see that the whole point of living free, of sharing, of not building barns for tomorrow, is a direct response to the sovereignty and fatherhood of God. If God is God then things are for sharing. If you cling to them, gather them in around you, possess them, then your heart will be in them. So how we live, our lifestyle, is presented as the inevitable response to the sovereignty of God, and to lay that direct reference to God aside is to reduce a joyful response to a studied technique for solving social problems. Nor do I think that Christians and humanists really meet each other truthfully if either of them deny what really makes them what they are. They just end up with an impotent common factor.

Another example: when people talk about non-violent action they often convert response into technique. For Christ it was essential to use non-violence entirely because it was truth he was preaching, and truth must be its own support, its own defence, and not bring in other defence to secure it; indeed if it does, then it destroys its own presentation. So for Christ, non-violence with its ultimate vulnerability to the forces of evil, was necessary because of the content of his Gospel. But so often today you hear it spoken of as a technique for achieving one's aims better than other people; one could use such non-violent techniques for selling soap better than one's opponents.

Another aspect of domestication: there is around today a very naive understanding of suffering and joy as though the two were opposites. I think this does affect some of our charity thinking. That all suffering is evil and that all welfare is good and that the task is to convert suffering into welfare somehow. This is a very naive interpretation of the human condition, of what suffering really is, of what joy really is. All of us know in our experience that the people we've met who have the deepest and profoundest joy very often know what real suffering is, because in suffering they have plummeted depths of human experience that you or I probably never plummet because we live today on the surface of things, and are constantly encouraged to do so.

In Northern Ireland for instance if you live in Belfast for a while, or talk to people from there, although the great tragedy of human life and death, of good and evil, is very present, you also discover the sparks of a terrific determination to live, the conviction that things can be other than they are, and that humour is always possible.

One suspects that usually in human history real beginnings of new life have come from profound experiences of suffering and not from the rather superficial experiences of life that we have in our Western climate. How superficial this experience is came home to me when we called our oil shortage before Christmas a 'crisis'. I was hard put to know how you put this over to people from the pulpit. It occurred to me that you can either say 'My dear brethren, you have no idea how much more it's going to cost to heat the church' and 'isn't life hard and we've got to face this'. Or, you learn a lesson from the prophets in the Old Testament that times of famine, starvation, persecution are moments of truth in which you look again at who you are; you learn to repent. It's a new birth, new life. I think this is important, and I think that most of us here, although we called that a crisis, knew it really wasn't one and it's nothing to what we're going to have to face in the next ten years in this country.

Many of the presuppositions on which our society has rested for the last 100 years or so are going to give way. We're going to have to learn how to interpret this to people. Is it a moment for self pity and bitterness about those horrible people over there who are destroying our lives or is it a moment of truth in which we come back to some basis of human life and learn to be humans again and learn that we can live rather better with less?

The last thing I'd like to say about domesticating the Gospel is: realize that when Christ preached his message he warned them that he would cause conflict, that he would divide people, that he would separate mother from daughter, father from son, that the peace he brought wasn't the sort of peace that the world offers, it was the sort of peace that would send them to their deaths and persecution. In other words, his peace in linked with being a sign of contradiction in the world. He is warning them that if they seek Truth and are faithful, then they will find, indeed cause, conflict.

Let me read to you a little piece from a book called *Return to the Source* by Lanza del Vasto. He was a count, who left everything to walk to the source of the Ganges. He was a fine Christian and in his diary he reflects on the Indian gods, explaining why statues show the gods dancing and tearing people to pieces at the same time. But he says of Brahma, the god above all gods: 'Brahma does not dance and I have never heard of him tearing anybody to pieces. That is why everybody speaks of him with respect but nobody prays to him and nobody adores him'. I sometimes suspect that we could slip in our modern Christian Christ into that text. So to finish with I'd like to read you the beginning and the end of a poem by William Blake, called the *Everlasting Gospel*:

'The vision of Christ that thou dost see
Is my vision's greatest enemy:
Thine has a great hook nose like thine,
Mine has a snub nose like to mine:
Thine is the friend of all mankind,
Mine speaks in parables to the blind:
Thine loves the same world that mine hates,
Thy Heaven doors are my Hell gates.
Both read the Bible day and night,
But thou read'st black where I read white.'

Then the long poem questions whether Christ was a nice polite person, and finds that he was outspoken to colleagues, challenged authorities, and confronted accepted norms. The poem ends:

'I'm sure this Jesus will not do,
Either for Englishman or Jew.'

FROM 'THE REFUGEES' by EDWIN MUIR

A crack ran through our hearthstone long ago,
And from the fissure we watched gently grow
The tame domesticated danger,
Yet lived in comfort in our haunted rooms.
Till came the Stranger
And the great and the little dooms...

We did not fear
A wrong so dull and old,
So patiently told and patiently retold,
While we sat by the fire or in the window-seat.
Oh what these suffered in dumb animal patience,
That we now suffer,
While the world's brow grows darker and the world's hand
    rougher.
We bear the lot of nations,
Of times and races,
Because we watched the wrong
Last too long
With non-commital faces.
Until from Europe's sunset hill
We saw our houses falling
Wall after wall behind us,
What could blind us
To such self-evident ill
And all the sorrows from their caverns calling?

This is our punishment. We came
Here without blame, yet with blame,
Dark blame of others, but our blame also.
This stroke was bound to fall,
Though not to fall so.
A few years did not waste
The heaped up world. The central pillar fell
Moved by no living hand. The good fields sickened
By long infection. Oh this is the taste
Of evil done long since and always, quickened
No one knows how
While the red fruit hung ripe upon the bough
And fell at last and rotted where it fell.

For such things homelessness is ours
And shall be others'. Tenement roofs and towers
Will fall upon the kind and the unkind
Without election,
For deaf and blind
Is rejection born by rejection
Breeding rejection,
And where no counsel is what will be will be.
We must shape here a new philosophy.

THE DINOSAUR, CHAMELEONS
AND WASPS

(A letter to a student)

Dear John,

Thank you for your letter, which I have tried to take in. I am going to assume the basic question you ask is: How are you to be faithful to God in the present situation you, and we, are in?

You remark that you feel distanced from your own parents not merely by a quarter century difference of age but also a whole shift of interpretation of life and how to respond to God. I should be careful not to let that distance turn either into arrogance, on one hand, nor into a feeling of guilt, on the other — I mean blaming yourself for not finding it easy to communicate with those you love. Rather I should seek prayerfully to appreciate what it is that separates; sometimes I feel that a fault line as in strata has appeared in our Christian language and faith, so that Christians on either side seem to use the same words, same strata, but simply do not connect.

But first let's think of where we seem to be just now in our society. You liken the situation to that of a great wave breaking. I like the picture: A great wave coming up the beach, building up, confident in its own strength and hardly noticed by those floating on top, until the critical moment when spume appears on the crest and the whole wave overrides itself, breaks and collapses, tossing whoever floated on it into chaos — except for the few who know the laws of its breaking well enough to be carried very fast and gently to shore.

This 'threshold point' is to be found in the development of many human organizations, not only at the large scale of modern society as a whole. The size and complexity of organization slowly become, without those involved really noticing, the major factor which prevents life and warm-blooded, convivial, creativity. You know, for instance, enough of my own monastic community to see that this is one of the trickiest situations to resolve. Possible openings to the future come up, or would, which in a smaller less complex setting could be mastered, shared and either given a joyful 'yes' or joyful 'no'; but beyond a critical size and complexity these openings prove not only difficult but impossible; they flounder in the actual process of trying to master them. This is not only a shame but destructive because it demoralizes. 'Hope deferred makes the heart grow sick' (Proverbs). It is too easy a way out to blame this dulling process on individuals for being silly or afraid. It is to do with a complexity and size beyond which no member can reasonably comprehend and relate to the whole — which is perhaps the central characteristic of 'community'.

Well, you and I seem to agree, John, that our economic and social structures at large, today, have become so massive and so inter-dependent that no one feels he can comprehend the whole. This widespread feeling that we are all caught up in processes that are beyond anyone's control is what I understand is meant by alienation.

One aspect of this is the greater specialization that has been encouraged both in the work people do and in the subjects people study. I am sure you see at your University how, in recent decades, each person has studied and knows more and more about less and less; heading perhaps towards knowing all about nothing?

But at the same time as this greater specialization we are increasingly aware of what is going on in the world, because of the amazing explosion in communications. Radio, T.V., newsprint, thrust us into immediate acquaintance with all and everything in our global village. I say 'acquaintance' because I don't think we comprehend and absorb and interpret most news; it is news not truth, and for this reason can help to make us feel immensely powerless.

Another aspect of the same thing is to think of the food and other things we buy and consume. Two centuries ago these would have come from local areas and by local processes easily understood and known. But now each of us is a meeting-point of vast and complex lines of production and processing which connect us as closely with the tin miner in Bolivia or the sugar cane family in Jamaica, as with the grocer in the shopping centre. We are all involved, we cannot have any choice about it, and we know that the whole intricate system works constantly into the hands of the well-off countries and the well-off within our own country.

Well we have known about all this for some time, but now there is something new in the air: I mean the general feeling that it-won't-go-on-like-this. It was not many years ago that we still had a feeling that we'd never had it so good and all the graphs could go on up and up indefinitely. But I think we are beginning to see that as a fool's paradise, and certainly I would think that the innate violence within our economic and political behaviour (and indeed in our use of non-renewable resources) has not only shown itself but just about caught up with the system itself. I find that Edwin Muir's poem *The Refugees* catches superbly what I mean (I enclose a copy, it bears careful reflection).

Of course people hope that our present series of 'crises' will pass by and we shall all return to 'normal' again; but I think not. Whether the anger of those abroad who have provided endless cheap labour and endless cheap raw materials will at last convert them from yes-men into no-men, no longer at our beck and call to fill up our shops (and cars?); or whether we shall simply run out of natural resources, who knows? What seems certain to me is that a society so naively and wholly bent on material well-being can hardly find within itself the spiritual power to cut back.

I am inclined to think that many of what people point to as causes of our troubles, inflation, overt violence, or longer term things like the breakdown of family life, should be thought of rather as symptoms than as causes. Much easier of course to be able to point at them as causes, but I think for a person of faith they should be seen as symptoms and encourage us to look for more ultimate causes.

We stand, John, at a turning point of history, a point where familiar things either fall apart or seize up. We have got ourselves into the position of the dinosaur: an enormous growth and very powerful, having evolved under the logic of its own rules of growth, but alas no longer adaptable to its environment; the end point of a line of cold blooded animals which can only give way to the emergence of new lines of warm blooded animals, smaller and more adaptable.

So what shall we do?

There is a danger that fear and self hatred could render us powerless. For it is certainly true that the alienation involved in our situation affects everyone, not only the poor and the oppressed.

If St John will forgive a slight shift in what he meant by the beast: the dinosaur 'compels everyone — small and great, rich and poor, slave and citizen — to be branded . . . and makes it illegal for anyone to buy or sell anything unless he has been branded with the name of the beast'. And such is the over-all dominion claimed by the beast that people cry out in fear, even while committing themselves to it, 'Who can compare with the beast? who can free us from him?'

So what are we going to do?

In the first place let's recognize that situations are trapping and problems insoluble precisely because we view them from within. That is, we have been shaped not only in the way we live but also in the way we think and interpret life by the structure and society in which we grow up and live.

In this sense we are all chameleons, we become the situations in which we are. One often finds, for instance,

33

C

that people are defensive about their jobs and their particular work because they have been moulded by that work into a very limited interpretation of what life is all about, what the Church is, what man is.

I find, for instance, that I need a van in Warrington because I have one, not the other way round. T.V. makes people T.V.-dependent, continental holidays make people holiday-dependent. But in much more subtle ways we become locked in to our cultural addictions precisely because our whole interpretation of life, and the mental categories we have available to interpret who we are, where we can go, are formed by the culture in which we exist. We are chameleons.

But if our way of seeing is formed by our culture it is also true that our culture is formed by our way of seeing. As Churchill said of buildings, a propos rebuilding the House of Commons, 'We shape buildings and then buildings shape us'.

So Christians need, in great humility, to recognize that it was a particular Christian spirituality which encouraged the birth and nursed what has now grown into our dinosaur. I mean the privatised, achievement based, life-is-about-good-behaviour, interpretation of our relationship with God. It is with no lack of ecumenical sensitivity that we can all recognize ourselves as wasps, white Anglo-Saxon Protestants. We are all, in our various Christian traditions and in various different ways, involved. We have allowed ourselves to use the Gospel for our own ends, instead of seeing that it sheds a critical light upon us.

So what are we going to do? If we are chameleons and wasps, because of the particular cultural and historical situation in which God has placed us, what is he asking us to do?

To say: 'There is nothing we can do, or to take on a great guilt or self-hatred at finding ourselves willy nilly involved in immensely unjust structures' is perhaps the ultimate blasphemy and despair. Heavy guilt, unlike awareness of sin, is never 'of God' because it is not creative, and while it is true that we are conditioned, like chamelons, it is also true that we have within us the divine spirit capable of standing clear of our situation, seeing it with other eyes and moving forward into creative new alternatives. To see things as they are, within an ultimate and not localised context, is nine-tenths of being set free. This is why John spoke of truth setting us free and of faith overcoming the world.

We certainly need each of us, to open ourselves in obedience to be formed by the word of God, his word spoken to us in our liturgy, in the scriptures, and in the living tradition of our community faith (the Church). This is what obedience is all about, a word so debased by organizational or stoic overtones. It really means, *ob-audire,* the art of having ears to hear, an openness to be formed by God's word. It is a feminine reflective virtue, not a tough masculine one. And it should free us from that privatised picking and choosing which one often hears in ecumenical talk: I can't take that, I can take this, this is how we do it, that's not our thing. People get locked into local 'opinions' and 'persuasions' and not set free by a search for truth.

In fact, you know, we find this obedience in the life of Christ. Two things have struck me recently about him:

35

(a) how totally was his mind formed by scripture, so that his interpretation of life and of his own mission was in terms of the prophets, the psalms and other Old Testament writings, and (b) how much his own response to the will of his Father was in the concrete situation of his own cultural and social moment of history. I think our customary theological language of him being God and man has obscured something of who he really was, and the extent to which he studied the art of knowing his Father's will in his concrete, existential setting. What revealed God in Christ was the way in which he was man.

So likewise if we are to be Christ in our situation we need to be formed by God's word and also take seriously the moment of history in which we actually exist. The former of these is not primarily an intellectual process but a whole-person process leading to us knowing God in the scriptural sense as a husband 'knows' his wife. Although study is an important part, such knowledge of God's word and will must involve authentic prayer and the ability to withdraw from the immediate scene of life.

I say 'authentic prayer' because we can kid ourselves. Not all prayer activity is authentic Christian prayer. Last summer eight of us from my community were staying at a Cistercian monastery in Northern Ireland. Late one night — no, early one morning — we had been discussing monastic prayer and the Abbot had listened quietly for sometime to these Benedictines when he said, very thoughtfully, 'of course we need to have some criteria to assess whether our prayer really is prayer at all. And I think one of these criteria must be: Do I find that my prayer is changing my life? If it is not, then it probably isn't prayer at all, if it is, then perhaps it is prayer'. It is quite possible that our prayer conforms us to our world and does not lay us open to the word of God. The pharisees were great pray-ers.

I think, John, that I'm suspicious of some current approaches to meditation. They can so easily turn us in on our own thoughts and conform us instead of forming us. Authentic Christian prayer must open us to the will and the mind of God. Julian of Norwich says 'Prayer oneth the soul to God', and such a one-ing can hardly be a safe and consoling experience, for our God is one with whom we must tussle, be knocked down, be picked up, and to know him will prove fairly subversive in society, certainly risky, and never quite satisfying in human terms, though of course it creates in us that real inner peace, that shalom, that one-ness within ourself, which is the unique gift of' God-who-is-one, and which is quite other than coming to terms with our world.

But then I also find I am a little suspicious of the excited 'Jesus saves' approach to prayer. It can so easily destroy the inner mystery of God, known-as-unknown, revealed in and yet beyond the man Jesus. If that mystery is removed, people catch a sort of alternative enthusiasm which lets them off seeking God's saving and liberating work within their own real world. But I do think that Jesus-saves is far more healthy a starting point for the Christian pilgrim than an excessive emphasis on Christ as God, in a static, all-is-well, sort of way.

To put all this simply perhaps we can say: God's word does not only speak, but it speaks to us in our concrete 1975 situation. This is why our 'encounter into God' must involve knowledge of who we are, what does it mean to be us.

The question: Who am I? has three orbits of answer. I am me as an individual person, I am me in my immediate social and community relations, and I am me involved in the wider structures and historical processes. By and large Christian spirituality and theology have been concerned with God's presence, his grace, in the first of these three.

MY LORD

Our mystics for instance wrote in a very personalised way; and the history of theology is largely a story of how God is present to the individual, veering from the Pelagian excess (I can cope O.K. thanks) on one side, to the Lutheran (I'm a nobody) on the other. This is why we have inherited a very privatised idea of man; we think of property as simply mine (rather than part of my relationship with others and the whole), we think of freedom as me threatened by others (rather than freedom residing precisely in my relations with others), we think of rights likewise rooted in the self (the U.N. declaration expressing a very privatised waspish interpretation of human rights).

For much the same reasons our spirituality is also dualistic, the real me being a ghost in a machine, not a whole body-soul person. I suspect this is one reason why the whole industrial capitalist complex could grow up largely unchallenged by the gospel; men of faith were concerned with an inner spiritual life more or less detached from life's physical and social wholeness.

You find this same inner sanctum idea of the gospel in many very good Christians, whose 'Christianity' is felt to make no demands on their practical decisions or style of life, they are concerned with Truth, not truth-lived.

Even in our monastic world we have suffered from this private, inner-me, spirituality. If ever there was an interpretation of life in its totality it was the monastic one, in which every element of life is seen, not as neutral, but either saying 'yes' or 'no' to the kingdom of God. I would think that most of our real renewal in monasteries is trying to recapture this life-in-its-entirety and grow away from the inner/outer dualism that has bugged us so long.

OUR LORD

Our background, then, gives us a fairly developed sense of God's grace at work in the person, and thus also a sense of personal sin (God always reveals sin in the context of grace-that-can-free). We have a less well-developed, but now growing, sense of God's grace in our communities. Most of our liturgical renewal is towards recapturing a sense of God-dwelling-in-his-people, as a people, so that we gather for worship and prayer not as a suitable setting for private prayers, but precisely as a community which is a locus for communal grace and communal sin.

LORD OF HISTORY

But perhaps our greatest challenge today is at the third orbit, of structures and historical processes.

I know, John, that you have a keen sense of being involved in social structures, and I know that you realize that every structure is both just and unjust in the way it works things out for people (that is necessarily true of every structure). That part of the answer to: Who am I? is this involvement in structures and life-styles which we find ourselves in rather than opting for, and which we know to dominate the lives of most people, is part of the awareness of many people today, especially perhaps among students. And this third range of awareness has been much encouraged in the last twelve years by documents from the Vatican Council, the Pope and the Synod of Bishops.

The challenge lies in the fact that our spirituality has not caught up with this awareness, we have not learnt to interpret it in terms of faith and the kingdom of God. And the result is that people feel anxious, or guilty, or simply lost, being laboured and heavy burdened without any opening to the future. So how are we to interpret this third range of structural, political awareness?

Well, if there is such a thing as structural sin which we are aware of as working against life and the kingdom, then it must also be true that there is structural grace, because God only reveals sin, and calls us to *metanoia*, a change of heart-and-life, in the context of his saving action. We need to recover a deep sense of God as Lord of history, to experience it, dwell on it, bring it into our prayer (it is already in the liturgy!) and so come to discover that God is at work not only in the individual person, not only in the local community of family, monastery, neighbourhood, but also in the structural or 'societal' movements which affect our lives. He is at work within historical processes as such, he is Lord of history, *our* history, John.

In scripture we find this, or elements of it, in the prophets and the Book of Revelation. But, John, beware: As you study and pray this new level of awareness, as it changes from head-knowledge to heart-knowledge, as it changes from a notional assent to a real assent, as you appropriate to yourself what had previously been external knowledge, you will find yourself seeing and feeling in quite new ways. And this will estrange you, perhaps painfully, from the thinking of many of your friends, from many people you know to be good and holier than yourself. And sooner or later will make demands on what you do/don't do, with your life.

Your love for people will gain what can only be called a dimension of 'political love'. Don't be suspicious that this is any the less authentic Christian love than your immediate interpersonal love. But you will find it harder to live with, and more difficult to live out in practice, and requiring greater staying power and inner peace, than the latter.

Somehow we must hold in balance our knowledge that structural change is essential if the oppressed are to be set free, and yet know that no system will ever be just, nor relieve us from the demands of daily love and caring. I think that both Vinoba Bhave and T.S. Eliot are right:

'We do not aim at doing acts of kindness, but at creating a kingdom of kindness'.

and 'We constantly try to escape
      From the darkness outside and within
      By dreaming of systems so perfect that no one will
          need to be good.'

Years ago, Ignatius of Antioch remarked that what authenticates the gospel is not that it is welcomed by the world but that it is rejected by it; certainly this was the clear warning of Christ. Seek truth and expect trouble. We are now in times somewhat like the early Christians,

41

and if the Christian is to withdraw from his cultural addictions I think he should expect withdrawal symptoms. Not least of these is the fear that his withdrawal is irresponsible and rather silly. But in all this, John, see your own search as part of God's gift to you, given for others; it is part of the Church's struggle to appropriate into herself new ways of saying yes to almighty God; you are the Church, so however meaningless much of what you find in established Christian practice, don't feel you're less really the Church than anyone else.

When a ray of light passes through a prism it splays out into a whole spectrum from red at one end to blue at the other. In some ways that is what has happened to Christians, certainly to Catholics, in the last decade or so. We have to learn to hold on to Christ as our centre of unity, while finding ourselves with many disparate understandings of truth.

I have written too long and must stop, but in all practical matters, John, do work to enhance and build up small-scale warm-blooded alternatives to the cold-blooded dinosaur. I find the emergence of such in our society one of the most encouraging signs of the work of the Spirit. People refusing to wait around for others to solve their problems, the sort of welfare-will-solve-all moral depression that is so rife, but taking hold of their own situation and saying 'come on we can do it'.

This is found in community action, it is found in our celebration of the liturgy, it is found in many groups who decide that the world is at their feet if they decide it is.

After quite a long discussion with one of the young men helping to run the Bogside Community Association in Derry, when he had explained their fed-up-ness with all outsiders claiming the ability to sort things out, whether politicians, I.R.A., or whoever, and how they had decided to take life and the future into their own hands and build their own future and community, one of our monks said 'And what would we need in Britain to discover these lessons for ourselves?' With an Irish smile he answered: 'To go through something like what we have been through'.

I suspect, John, that what God asks of us is all contained in that beautiful phrase of the prophet Micah: 'Act justly, love tenderly, walk humbly with your God'.

Shalom,

Thomas.

P.S. I enclose a passage from another Cistercian, Thomas Merton, which powerfully warns against the domesticating influence of prayer wrongly understood. I wonder what had happened in his community to make him write it?

*   *   *

'SINCE YOU SAY "WE SEE", YOUR GUILT REMAINS' (John 9)

All methods of meditation that are, in effect, merely devices for allaying and assuaging the experience of emptiness and dread are ultimately evasions which can do nothing to help us. Indeed, they may confirm us in delusions and harden us against that fundamental awareness of our real condition, against the truth for which our hearts cry out in desperation.

What we need is not a false peace which enables us to evade the implacable light of judgement, but the grace courageously to accept the bitter truth that is revealed to us; to abandon our inertia, our egoism and submit entirely to the demands of the Spirit, praying earnestly for help, and giving ourselves generously to *every effort asked of us by God.*

A method of meditation or a form of contemplation that merely produces the illusion of having 'arrived somewhere', of having achieved security and preserved one's familiar status by playing a part, will eventually have to be unlearned in dread — or else we will be confirmed in the arrogance, the impenetrable self-assurance of the Pharisee. We will become impervious to the deepest truths. We will be closed to all who do not participate in our illusion. We will live 'good lives' that are basically inauthentic, 'good' only as long as they permit us to remain established in our respectable and impermeable identities. The 'goodness' of such lives depends on the security afforded by relative wealth, recreation, spiritual comfort, and a solid reputation for piety. Such 'goodness' is preserved by routine and the habitual avoidance of serious risk — indeed of serious challenge. In order to avoid apparent evil, this pseudo-goodness will ignore the summons of genuine good. It will prefer routine duty to courage and creativity. In the end it will be content with established procedures and safe formulas, while turning a blind eye to the greatest enormities of injustice and uncharity.

Such are the routines of piety that sacrifice everything else in order to preserve the comforts of the past, however inadequate and however shameful they may be in the present. Meditation, in such a case, becomes a factory for alibis and instead of struggling with the sense of falsity and inauthenticity in oneself, it battles against the exigencies of the present, armed with platitudes minted in the previous century. If necessary, it also fabricates condemnations and denunciations of those who risk new ideas and new solutions.

(Thomas Merton, *The Climate of Monastic Prayer,* Ch. XVII)

WHERE IS YOUR GOD?

(Based on a talk given to Oscott College, Birmingham, May 1975)

In his poem, *The Rock,* T.S. Eliot catches the insecurity latent in times of security, the it-can't-happen-to-us-illusion:

It is hard for those who have never known persecution,
And who have never known a Christian,
To believe these tales of Christian persecution.
It is hard for those who live near a Bank
To doubt the security of their money.
It is hard for those who live near a Police Station
To believe in the triumph of violence.
Do you think that the Faith has conquered the world
And that lions no longer need keepers?
Do you need to be told that whatever has been, can still be?
Do you need to be told that even such modest attainments
As you can boast in the way of polite society
Will hardly survive the Faith to which they owe their significance?
Men! polish your teeth on rising and retiring;
Women! polish your fingernails:

You polish the tooth of the dog and the talon of the cat.
Why should men love the Church? Why should
they love her laws?
She tells them of Life and Death, and of all that
they would forget.
She is tender where they would be hard, and hard
where they like to be soft.
She tells them of Evil and Sin, and other unpleasant
facts.
They constantly try to escape
From the darkness outside and within
By dreaming of systems so perfect that no one will
need to be good.
But the man that is will shadow
The man that pretends to be.
And the Son of Man was not crucified once for all,
The blood of martyrs not shed once for all,
The lives of Saints not given once for all:
But the Son of Man is crucified always
And there shall be Martyrs and Saints.

Now in our Christian spirituality we are relatively good
at interpreting times of personal suffering in terms of faith.
We know that personal faith only matures in the successive experience of both joy and suffering. Because God is
not to be trapped by our own experience and interpretation
of him, we need to experience both his presence and his
absence if we are to grow into the fullness of Christ.

But we are less used to interpreting the same ebb and
flow in the wider context of our social history. And there
is thus a temptation when things fall apart socially and
culturally not to find God and liberation, but to lose him.
Times of disintegration when men jeer at the believer:

now where is your God? are in fact moments of history when the hearts of many are laid bare. The central question becomes, once again, that of Christ: will faith be found upon earth? You will hear rumours of war, nation rising against nation, and even men of faith will be lured after this or that, but fear not. It is then that the Son of Man is to be found.

Nothing of course stimulates doom quicker than prophets of doom, nothing stimulates crisis quicker than those who shout fire! But what should one do when one thinks, as I happen to, that we face a breakdown which has built up slowly over a far longer period than we care to admit — 'we watched the wrong last too long with non-committal faces'?

It would be irresponsible to take a spectator or let's-pretend attitude, in the hope that if we don't open our eyes maybe it will all pass away. So what do we say?

*   *   *

Most of our present day prophets of doom diagnose the situation and offer various prognoses merely in economic and political terms. And in these terms doom is pretty depressing.

For many decades decisions have been made in our world by and for those with financial power. Trade relations internationally (the prices we pay for and the amount we buy of primary products) have been settled by the rich nations. Wage levels and employment intra-nationally have been settled by those with economic power. In both cases those with power have set standards of consumption and living which the natural resources of the world and the economic order we operate could never conceivably make available for everyone. In other words those in power have lived in a sort of dream world.

Now we face the new and surely to be expected advent of those who have so far been used as objects of other men's decisions starting to say 'us too, please', but not only to say it but also discover that they have power if they care to use it — the power to call the tune themselves, as the Arabs did over the price of oil (and others will do with other products?), or the unions do at home by withholding labour (which is the basis of the pathetic game being played out just now).

So we face the prospect of everyone not only wanting to, but increasingly having the power to, clamber on to the bandwagon which cannot conceivably take the load. And to look for merely economic or political solutions is short term patchwork because our economic problems are only the symptoms of the much deeper spiritual and cultural malaise of our technological go-getting society. Our life really is more than food and clothing and the urge to raise our food and clothing standards is only the symptom of a far deeper longing for life itself.

* * *

So, as things fall apart, what do we do? Certainly fear will increase among people with all its side effects of finding scapegoats or more fearful still retreating into left or right wing fascism. And many too will have that quite impotent, rather pained, innocent-victim reaction which refuses to accept that we are all involved and that we cannot afford to escape facing the darkness within:

> This is our punishment. We came
> Here without blame, yet with blame,
> Dark blame of others, but our blame also.

What do we do? Well there is probably no answer to that because our first task must always be to see things anew, interpret them afresh. As the Eye, such the Object, said Blake. The future opens out only for those who will face the hurt and the pain of real *metanoia*, repentance. That is to turn over and back to the really simple and central things of life, and to turn with deliberate and light-hearted steps away from all the nonsense we have cluttered ourselves with. Things fall apart so that we have a chance once again to be men.

Let's listen in for a moment on John's dream of the downfall of the great city (Rev. 18):

Mourn, mourn for this great city
doomed as you are within a single hour.
There will be weeping and distress over her
among all the traders of the earth
when there is nobody to buy their cargoes of goods;
their stocks of gold and silver;
wine, oil, flour and corn;
their stocks of cattle, sheep, horses,
their slaves, their human cargo.
'All the fruits you had set your hearts on have failed you;
gone forever, never to return, is your life of
    magnificence and ease'.
All the captains and seafaring men,
sailors and all those making a living from the sea
will be keeping a safe distance, watching and crying out
'Has there ever been a city as great as this!'
'Mourn, mourn for this great city
whose lavish living has made a fortune
for every owner of a sea-going ship;
ruined within a single hour.

49

'Now heaven, celebrate her downfall,
and all you saints, apostles and prophets:
God has given judgment for you against her.'
(Then an angel said:)
'Your traders were the princes of the earth,
all the nations were under your spell.
In her you will find the blood of prophets and saints,
and all the blood that was ever shed on earth.'

We must not suppose that the anger of God is like a testy school-master whacking boys for being naughty. It is rather the inbuilt downfall of all human pursuits and especially of society at large, which are pursued for idolatrous ends, however 'innocently', out of keeping with the kingdom, that is with disregard for truth and goodness and beauty, for simplicity, and above all for people — for people as people and not the objects of other peoples' games. At the beginning of his letter to the Romans, Paul spells this out — how God has provided us with ample evidence of how to live truth and if we choose not to then we set up a world which has within it the seeds of its own downfall. And when Mary says in the Magnificat:

He has shown the power of his arm,
he has routed the proud of heart.
He has pulled down princes from their thrones
and exalted the lowly.
The hungry he has filled with good things,
the rich sent empty away

she is not making some pious wishful think but wondering at the ways in which God would work within the laws of history. The future belongs to the poor when they discover that it does.

*   *   *

Time was when another people felt that much of what they had stood for had been shaken, that the role they once had had crumbled (and a God-given role at that), that the cultural bonds which gave them a place and a sense of purpose and belonging had snapped. That was when the chosen people found themselves dispersed in exile.

The prophets took hold of this situation and interpreted it, converting despair and uprootedness into a liberating moment of truth. They spelt out the fidelity and mercy of God, how he was to be found, indeed re-found, in the death and disillusion of such times, so that by authentic repentance the people would open up into the future. What emerged was the whole theme of the suffering servant, how life would be reborn not inspite of but through death, that what seemed like death throes could in fact be birth pangs, and God would make all things new. We can hardly re-cap the whole subtlety and beauty of this message of liberation and hope, but do read the whole of Deutero-Isaiah, chapters 40-55 and 60-62.

It was this through-death-to-life mystery of accepted suffering which became for Christ his own interpretation of his messianic role. His absolute demands to see truth and press home the demands of absolute love built up that reaction of those in power, for whom such demands are always unbearable, which emerged in the crisis of his death. And it was that crisis which he interpreted in terms of the suffering servant and is at the centre of all subsequent Christian faith.

To whom does the future belong? Weep not for me, said Jesus to the women beside the way of the cross, but weep for yourselves and your children. If men reject the wood that is nevertheless green, what will happen to that which is dead? Whatever the apparent evidence, the future is mine, and whatever the apparent evidence the future is lost for those in apparent power — they had their moment of truth, of peace, of liberation, but they lost it, and terrible will be the pain of collapse as a result. Leave the dead to bury the dead, follow me.

And for us? The same. Whatever the apparent evidence the future belongs to those who really seek truth in charity in any situation, who remain confident of the power of the powerless, the power of the gentle, the repentant, the power of those who are voices for the voiceless, the power of poverty which knows how to laugh roundly at idols, the power of those who will stand by the intrinsic value of truth and love in themselves, without calling in the mercenaries of political game playing or armed force when faced with mini-deaths or death itself.

God is no spectator and if at times we experience him more as absent than present that is only to invite us once again to leave what is second rate and effete, for what is true and good and beautiful:

The world is charged with the grandeur of God.
  It will flame out, like shining from shook foil;
  It gathers to a greatness, like the ooze of oil
Crushed, Why do men then now not reck his rod?
Generations have trod, have trod, have trod;
    And all is seared with trade; bleared, smeared
        with toil;
    And wears man's smudge and shares man's smell:
        the soil
Is bare now, nor can foot feel, being shod.

And for all this, nature is never spent;
    There lives the dearest freshness deep down things;
And though the last lights off the black West went
    Oh, morning, at the brown brink eastward,
        springs —
Because the Holy Ghost over the bent
    World broods with warm breast and with ah!
        bright wings.

(Gerard Manley Hopkins)

VERSES FROM PSALM 9

I will praise you, Lord, with all my heart;
I will recount all your wonders.
I will rejoice in you and be glad,
and sing psalms to your name, O Most High.

You have checked the nations, destroyed the wicked;
you have wiped out their name for ever and ever.
The foe is destroyed, eternally ruined.
You uprooted their cities; their memory has perished.

But the Lord sits enthroned for ever.
He has set up his throne for judgment;
he will judge the world with justice,
he will judge the peoples with his truth.

Sing psalms to the Lord who dwells in Sion.
Proclaim his mighty works among the peoples;
for the Avenger of blood remembered them,
and has not forgotten the cry of the poor.

The nations have fallen in the pit which they made,
their feet caught in the snare they laid.
The Lord has revealed himself, and given judgment.
The wicked are snared in the work of their own hands.

Let the wicked go down among the dead,
all the nations forgetful of God.
For the needy shall not always be forgotten
nor the hopes of the poor be in vain.

Arise Lord, let men not prevail!
Let the nations be judged before you.
Lord, strike them with terror,
let the nations know they are but men.

Lord, why do you stand afar off
and hide yourself in times of distress?
The poor man is devoured by the pride of the wicked:
he is caught in the schemes that others have made.

For the wicked man boasts of his heart's desires;
the covetous blasphemes and spurns the Lord.

In his pride the wicked says: 'He will not punish.
There is no God.' Such are his thoughts.

His path is never untroubled;
your judgment is far from his mind.
His enemies he regards with contempt.
He thinks: 'Never shall I falter:
misfortune shall never be my lot.'

He crouches, preparing to spring,
and the helpless fall beneath his strength.
He thinks in his heart: 'God forgets,
he hides his face, he does not see.'

Arise then, Lord, lift up your hand!
O God, do not forget the poor!
Why should the wicked spurn the Lord
and think in his heart: 'He will not punish'?

But you have seen the trouble and sorrow,
you note it, you take it in hand.
The helpless trusts himself to you;
for you are the helper of the orphan.

Break the power of the wicked and the sinner!
Punish his wickedness till nothing remains!
The Lord is king for ever and ever.
The heathen shall perish from the land he rules.

Lord, you hear the prayer of the poor;
you strengthen their hearts; you turn your ear
to protect the rights of the orphan and oppressed:
so that mortal man may strike terror no more.

'AS THE EYE, SO THE OBJECT'

(*William Blake*)

(Given to Ecumenical Congress, Liverpool, October 1974)

One of the great classical portrayals of the Buddha shows him sitting in the normal lotus position with his left hand upturned, holding a begging bowl, and his right hand resting on the other knee with one finger pointing down to earth.

The left hand, the begging bowl, represents the need for enlightenment. The feminine ability to take in, to listen to, the word of God, in our Christian tradition. This comes to us through the scripture, through the tradition of our community of belief — the Church — and through our liturgy.

The other hand, resting, pointing down to earth, represents the need for us to be embedded and realistic in the human condition in which we find ourselves, what for the purposes of this paper we can call political realism. We cannot live anywhere other than where God has asked us to live.

Any man of faith can tell one that the tension set up between these two hands, the tension between the need for enlightenment and a serious appreciation of the world we are in, is bound to cause great suffering, great loneliness. It's the loneliness of a man who is in the world but not of it, the loneliness we find written into the New Testament which separated Christ out from the world in which he lived, and yet related him so closely to it. And the suffering is that of the cross, the suffering which belongs to a desire to live and to speak truth. 'Speak truth with love' St Paul said, and that in any world setting involves suffering, just as it drove Christ to the cross.

But if the tension between these two hands is acute, it is also the only creative tension we have available. It arises from our human condition and if we do not experience the tension it is probable that we are not living faith in the sense Christ spoke of it.

*   *   *

We can escape from this tension of living faith by taking the right hand of involvement, or the left hand of enlightenment, to the exclusion of the other. With the right hand, for instance, we can seek to be so relevant to our world that we finish up as humanists with a mere Christian overlay. This appears often in Christian writing, in which seeking to be very relevant in our contemporary world, people merely inject occasional Gospel quotations to show that they are yet Christians.

William Temple will forgive me if I say that the 'social Gospel' can often lead to this lack of faith: the 'with-it-ness' of Christians, desperately hoping to be acceptable to the world. They interpret the Gospel as no more than a problem solving machine for the human situations in which we find ourselves.

*   *   *

On the other left hand we can escape the tension of living faith by constructing for ourselves an alternative society, a special world of Christians who have set up something alternative to the world in which God has placed them. This has been a constant temptation for Christians down through the ages, very often born of great enthusiasm and good will and yet missing perhaps the central point of incarnation. I remember in discussions with clergy in an ecumenical group near our monastery, one member would often say: what we want is neither Capitalism nor Communism, what we want is Christianity — as though Christianity was a total system in the world which could be free of any other economic or political system. This is not what we find in the Gospels.

We can also create this special religious world by enthusiastic pietism. One mustn't be rude about this because so often a person's growth into authentic Christian faith starts with an enthusiasm which is excellent while it lasts but must grow into something fuller, more human and more divine. It seems that the early Christians lived through this period. Following on the resurrection and the gift of the Spirit at Pentecost, they went through a time of great awareness of the risen Christ and the life of the Spirit in the world. But with the years and decades passing, they came to see again that the call from Christ was not simply to celebrate a risen Christ, but to follow him through life and death to resurrection. They redis-covered the cross within their own history.

Again, we do a left handed escape from living faith, when we make Christ into a cult figure, when we put him at a distance in order to worship him at the expense of knowing him as a model for ourself. A lady asked, in a discussion recently, 'do you think we can say that we have within each of us the potential to be as Christ was?' I suggested that, with care for the context in which we say it, we must be able to answer simply 'yes'. In our Catholic tradition, however, we have tended in our liturgy to distance Christ, place him on a divine pedestal for adoration, and 'alienated' the liturgy as a result. We were 'present' at, we 'attended', we 'heard' Mass, but somehow we did not celebrate Mass ourselves; it was done by the priest, done by the choir, and we were there as individuals in a privileged and attractive setting for our private prayer. And the presence of Christ in the Eucharist was distanced from us, made into a presence in its own right, a miraculous presence isolated from the rest of life, rather than being the focusing and celebrating of God's presence in all people, at all times and everywhere. It *is* right and fitting that we should always and everywhere give thanks.

Perhaps a vivid awareness that 'God is with us', that the primary answer to 'where is Christ' must always be 'in his people' (for his special Eucharistic presence only makes sense within this primary presence in people), perhaps this disarming humility of God is so unbearable to us that we always try in some way to distance God from us either by distancing Christ into a cult figure, and thus an idol, or in the opposite way by reducing him merely to a good man and useful teacher.

The dignity of the believer, and every man, is an awesome and demanding thing. No words sum it up more succinctly than those of the Son of God, after his resurrection through death: 'My God is your God, my Father is your Father'. And yet deep in the human psyche is the need to distance our God, and so unbearable are the implications of taking Christ as he actually gave himself to us, abandoning all role, all cult, that we release ourselves from the tension by placing him on a pillar. Christ's own faith was Theo-centric, but Christians so often make their faith Christo-centric. We have to rediscover again and again the spirituality set out by authentic liturgy; Christ is him with whom, and in whom and through whom we are drawn into union with the Father.

Our Catholic Eucharistic prayers avoid reference to Christ as God in order to preserve this dynamism of Christ being him in whom we are incorporated into God. But such is the human desire to alienate God that when people slip in their own acclamations after the consecration, they say 'My Lord and my God' or 'Venite adoremus', giving Christ's presence a nuance not found in the four original acclamations.

Christ's central invitation to us is not to adore him but to be Christ in our situation, and this is what we have to learn as Christians in each time, in each place down through history. To be Christ in our situation.

When St Paul spoke of Christ as being the true likeness of the God we cannot see, he wasn't talking of Christ being a photograph but he was talking of Christ being an icon, and an icon is a picture which points beyond itself. Its staring eyes invite us to go through itself to the God who is known as unknown, and a Christian faith that loses the mystery of God beyond, has not understood the strange mystery of the incarnation. He whom we can call Father because we are brothers with Christ, is yet the God whom we know as unknown. We should not say 'Jesus Christ frees and unites' but 'God who freed and united Jesus, his Son, also frees and unites us in Jesus Christ'.

*   *   *

We can also miss the tension of faith, the tension between that which is given (the left hand) and that which is lived in the world (the right), if we separate these two into exclusive compartments, and never allow the light received really to shine on and change what we do in the political reality in which we live. Each of our churches are guilty of this in different ways. We Roman Catholics have tended towards a privatised spirituality which has considered man as related to God, essentially in some inner spiritual life, and not in the totality of his human existence. This gives rise to many failures to live out the Gospel, to translate truth into life. It also domesticates the Gospel, taming the wild animal that we were given.

The Church of England perhaps has its own problems from being an established church. This has certainly conformed its spirituality to the society in which we live, just because of its equation with that society.

And the free churches have their own historical involvement in the growing up of the whole social, capitalist system in which we are all involved and in which we have to free ourselves. Manchester and Liverpool grew up under a particular understanding of human life and society in which free church spirituality had a part to play.

Whether we have privatised faith, or whether we have

61

baptized success (which perhaps in practice come to much the same thing), we have all been responsible for allowing our economic order to develop more or less free of the critical light which faith should cast upon it. Religious men, involved with themselves and their God, allowed our contemporary social and economic worlds to be shaped by the go-getters and the entrepreneurs. And the Church has thus got into the position of a dear man who stands at a 'T' junction outside a pub near Warrington, called the Fiddle in the Bag. He directs the traffic, and as each car appears he sees which way it wants to go and directs it in that direction. The drivers smile at him, and he smiles back, with a great sense of importance. He is popular and very 'relevant' but in fact does nothing at all.

*   *   *

What then is the Church? Is it an organization of people who are saved and safe, snatched from a wicked world which is nothing but a dangerous ambush? Such a model for the Church hardly recognizes that the world is God's creation and that the Christian is committed to loving all creation by celebrating his God in bread and wine.

A definition of the Church increasingly familiar in Catholic circles, and recovered from the early fathers, is that she is the universal sacrament of salvation. That is she points to, makes clear, articulates, enhances the unrecognized work of salvation and freedom and life which God is achieving in the lives of all people, at all times and everywhere.

I like to think of the Church as a crystal, suspended in the middle of liquid. There is nothing in the crystal which is not latent within the liquid itself, and yet it makes that known drawing its own life and vigour from that which is present in the whole of the liquid. The Church speaks to the world of its own reality, it speaks to the world of what is the real and ultimate significance of what is going on throughout the world and in all people.

This may sound charming, and gentle and attractive, but it is also cutting and prophetic and unwelcome, because as the sacrament of salvation, the Church must maintain her prophetic role. While being in the world she must also be over against it, in order to show up the critical nature of many things going on in the world of which we are not otherwise aware. It is urgent on us today to seek truth, to see things as they really are, to lay ourselves bare to the very painful process of coming to terms with who we are, where we are and what is taking place.

*   *   *

Let's now return to our original picture of the Buddha and the tension between the gift of revelation, essentially given and the political realism necessary for us to live and take seriously the world in which God has placed us.

If we understand this tension, then we know what Christ meant when he called himself the light of the world. He is not saying that in the past, people had no light and that now they have a light to look at. What he is saying is that he is the Light which illuminates the world, shows it up as what it really is, highlights the highlights and deepens the shadows. It is through our receiving the word of God, his revelation to us, that we are able to be realistic in the world in which he has placed us. This is very like the two sides of the dialectic of which

63

Hegel spoke: That which is taken for granted, the thesis as it were, challenged and illuminated by the antithesis; with the tension between these two creating the way forward. What he called the synthesis.

Similar too, to the now classic system of Cardinal Cardijn — See, Judge and Act. It is the Light of the world illuminating our situation which enables us to be free from that situation, to move forward. Much of our faith and the Gospel, is not to do with behaving well but learning to see things properly. In this sense it is liberating, because it frees us from those illusions which build up in ourselves as a result of our particular social setting. Through our education, through the culture in which we live, we learn to see things in a particular way. But we only half see things; and our minds are filled with illusions in which we see things in the way that is suitable for our culture. A culture defends itself and secures its own future by creating in our minds and the minds of all, illusory ways of interpreting life, of interpreting one another, of interpreting the world, which are in keeping with that particular culture. That is why so many problems appear to us insoluble because our minds are formed by the same processes which gave rise to the problems, and if we are not willing to be freed from the illusions that are in us then we have no means of transcending our situation, transcending the world and moving forward in faith. All that is left to us is despair.

It's my suspicion that many involved in social work of various kinds are trapped by hopelessness. Unless we have a vision beyond that in which we are involved, what we are involved in can produce nothing but despair. Hence the feeling amongst people that there is 'nothing we can do about it', there is no solution. All we can do is trundle along and hope that things don't get worse. But revelation rightly understood, if we truly understand Christ as the Light of the world, should set us free in our situation, not by solving our problems but by shedding a light upon them which gives us a different context and a new point of view, in the precise sense.

When Christ says that with faith we can move mountains, it may be that the mountains we thought existed in fact no longer exist at all. But quite certainly Christ did not come to solve people's problems. Indeed he created them, and he made it clear, especially to those in authority, that their problems would have been less if he had not come. The peace that he is offering them is not a peace through the solution of problems, but a peace which is beyond that, and which cuts away human death and suffering at a much deeper level.

Christ's only promise to the apostles, if they wished to follow him, was that they too would go through the process of rejection, of misunderstanding, of suffering and the cross. Their hope had to be in God himself, and not in the expected solution to national and social problems. This is not because he was disinterested in social problems, but because within their own context they are insoluble.

*   *   *

Now each of us has illusions about different things. We have illusions about oneself, our pride, our sense of ego, our sense of importance. We cling to these for our security, albeit, a false security. We have illusions about the immediate communities in which we live. In my

65

particular involvement with the Justice and Peace Commission, the illusions we have been involved in are those on the wider social scene, those to do with the political nature of man — the illusions that each of us holds within us about the sort of society in which we live and have our future.

Elsewhere I have mentioned some of these illusions. The illusions about property — 'What's-mine-is-mine,-I-earned-it-didn't-I?' One only has to know the attitude towards things and ownership in other societies than our own to know how very limited is our approach to property and ownership. An African for instance is so intimately bound up with his own family (and family for him is an extended family, with uncles and aunts, and nephews and nieces, included) that if he earns anything, it belongs quite naturally and automatically to the family as a whole. To be himself is to be family.

There is the trickle-down illusion, the basic assumption so convenient to those who are well off, that as long as the well-off do better and better, then sooner or later it trickles down to everyone.

There is the things-are-good-or-things-are-bad illusion, from which Christ freed the rich by returning again and again to the fact that it is good things that are dangerous and that separate men from the kingdom.

The illusions that we have in our mind, are very closely connected to the idols which we go after, and idols are always in themselves good, not bad. They become distracting and preoccupying precisely because they are good and the human heart can go after them. Idols are good, but they are only secondary goods and are never in the end capable of satisfying the human heart. In addition idols are captivating because at each stage they prove disappointing. They tend to lead us on to assume that if at this step we haven't been satisfied, it is because we haven't taken the next one. This is true certainly of the three great idolatries of men. Of power, of property and of pleasure. But the answer to each of these is never to seek further in the hopes of attaining what is held out, because idols are illusory in the sence that they promise that which they intrinsically cannot supply. There is only one who is faithful to his promises and that is almighty God himself.

And so throughout the Gospels we find the sharp contrast between giving oneself to idols, in themselves good, but idols nonetheless, and to almighty God himself, through whom alone we can enjoy all things free of idolatry.

And then there is the insidious illusion of 'we're-us-they're-them', the 'we-and-they' illusion by which we secure ourselves in a known way of life and amongst known people, and are able mentally to cut ourselves off from those 'over there'. How many of the parables of Christ were a prophetic warning about this illusion within us. One recalls his little warning that when we give meals we are not to invite our friends and those we know, because then we have our rewards already. But we are to make a point of inviting those who are forgotten, those who are outcast, those who are not one of 'us'. All the way through the Gospel, the economy, as it were, is that we are to behave one to another as God behaves towards us. And if he has no distinctions between nice and nasty, (indeed if he did they would be the opposite way round to ours!) then who are we to make distinctions between us and them? Every man is my brother, because I am an adopted son of the Father of Christ.

*　　*　　*

There is a danger that we think of the process of clearing our minds and hearts of illusions, as a merely interior or intellectual one, but this is not so, because to know God and to be Christ in our situation, always involves life. This is in fact true of all authentic human knowledge. We don't know in a vacuum, and then live out what we know, but we discover and know in and out of the same process as making decisions about life. As Chuang Tsu, the Chinese philosopher, said: 'A path is made by those who walk upon it'.

St Paul urged us to preach the word, but for him it was the word of life, not a mere intellectual way of understanding things. All the way through the Gospels, Christ elicits faith from people, not by words but by inviting them to do something. His miracles of healing never took the form of a person being healed, discovering that, and then getting up and walking. The command was 'Get up and walk' and it was in the action that the healing took place.

Faith is not an interior, merely spiritual thing, it is a way of walking through life. Martin Buber pointed out that when Moses longed to find out from God what his true name was, in other words to fix God and have him clear, the real meaning of the answer that God gave was 'I am he who will be present in the obedient carrying out of what I am asking you to do'. In other words, through obedience you will discover God in the process of life.

Nowadays when people are so bored with Christian language and talk and words, how important it is that Christians should step forward in the process of discovering their own faith. This is why Christ would never give people a clear code of behaviour, because once they have a clear code of behaviour they no longer need faith. For a man to believe in God, and to behave in the only way in keeping with that faith, were to be one and the same thing. To know that we are loved by God, is one and the same as sharing that love with one another. To know that we are forgiven by God, is one and the same as learning to forgive one another. When people have a clear code of life, once they can answer the question 'what shall we do?', then faith is dead. Christ did not leave the apostles with a clear blueprint of what to do about the good news. Indeed he left them locked in an upper room for 40 or 50 days waiting for the inspiration that was the answer to that question. So for us, we must beware of looking for clear blueprints, or clear outlines of the future, before we move forward.

It is a great mistake for clergy (or parents or teachers) to suppose that we can supply, for all people universally, the answer to their problems. But we can show them Christ, and in showing them Christ, enable them to have within themselves a faith which finds its own path. Paths are made by those who walk upon them!

*　　*　　*

By way of conclusion then, let's ask the question 'Quo Vadis', where are we going, what can we do? The question that has no answers but is worth asking nevertheless. Perhaps we need to rediscover *Christian poverty*, not primarily as a way of solving our problems, but as a way of setting ourselves free from being trapped by the society in which we live. We cannot really know God without a discipline of life, without freeing ourselves from other worships in order to discover God himself. Poverty is a liberating and freeing thing, through which, surprise surprise, the whole world is ours.

We can look to our *prayer* and see if it is opening up to us the light of the world, and not conforming us to the world. Not all prayer activity is authentic Christian prayer.

We can try to understand the Gospel more in terms of *truth* than proper behaviour. Try to catch once again the Eastern and early Christian understanding that the basis of sin is in ignorance, of not seeing things rightly, of being blind. This process in our life will never be easy, it's a continuous and demanding process. We have to learn the art of engaging, of withdrawing, in order to engage again. But without withdrawal from the scene in which we are, we never come to see it for what it is. We need to withdraw to the desert or its equivalent. We need to withdraw to meet God in the burning bush, if we are to return to and see social things in a way that God would have us see them. All the Christian enthusiasm in the world will not replace the vision which comes from seeing things in the light of God. Today this process is one that few people can undertake alone. We need to learn the ways of praying, of meeting, of discussing together, in order that together we can come to see further than we do at present.

Again we can look at the *pattern of our lives* and see whether busyness and a certain self-importance and per-haps self-pity are not the very things that blind us into our situation. When Thomas More explained how it was that he had come to the way of seeing things that he had, he described this as the result of 'long leisure and patient diligence'. What a beautiful use of the word leisure, but how often in our lives it's the very element that is missing!

And lastly let us be quite certain, that if we are to pursue this course of seeing our world rightly, and living truth as a result, then we are going to need *hypomone,* that special Christian virtue of staying power, of patient endurance, buoyed up by a constant interplay between prayer and study and involvement.

I finish by leaving you with this one thought; that we live today in a time when it is far more important that Christians should see rightly than behave well.

PSALM 72 (73)

How good God is
to those who are pure of heart.
Yet my feet came close to stumbling,
my steps had almost slipped
for I was filled with envy of the proud
when I saw how the wicked prosper.

For them there are no pains;
their bodies are sound and sleek.
They have no share in men's sorrows;
they are not stricken like others.

So they wear their pride like a necklace,
they clothe themselves with violence.
Their hearts overflow with malice,
their minds seethe with plots.

They scoff; they speak with malice;
from on high they plan oppression.
They have set their mouths in the heavens
and their tongues dictate to the earth.

So the people turn to follow them
and drink in all their words.
They say: 'How can God know?
Does the Most High take any notice?'
Look at them, such are the wicked,
but untroubled, they grow in wealth.

*　　*　　*

How useless to keep my heart pure
and wash my hands in innocence,
when I was stricken all day long
suffered punishment day after day.

Then I said: 'If I should speak like that,
I should betray the race of your sons.'

I strove to fathom this problem
too hard for my mind to understand,
until I pierced the mysteries of God
and understood what becomes of the wicked.

*   *   *

How slippery the paths on which you set them;
you make them slide to destruction.
How suddenly they come to their ruin,
wiped out, destroyed by terrors.
Like a dream one wakes from, O Lord,
when you wake you dismiss them as phantoms.

And so when my heart grew embittered
and when I was cut to the quick,
I was stupid and did not understand,
no better than a beast in your sight.

Yet I was always in your presence;
you were holding me by your right hand.
You will guide me by your counsel
and so you will lead me to glory.

What else have I in heaven but you?
Apart from you I want nothing on earth.
My body and my heart faint for joy;
God is my possession for ever.

All those who abandon you shall perish;
you will destroy all those who are faithless.
To be near God is my happiness.
I have made the Lord God my refuge.
I will tell of all your works
at the gates of the city.

A PACK OF ILLUSIONS

'...... it is not the Lie, that passeth through the Minde, but the Lie that sinketh in, and setleth in it, that doth the hurt......' (*Francis Bacon,* ESSAYS 1625).

It will help to take a concrete example in which to locate some of our most cherished illusions. Last year in the Sahel, those countries which lie across Africa at the southern edge of the Sahara, a drought took the lives of between one and two hundred thousand people, and because of severe malnutrition in early months may have permanently damaged the growth of many more children.

We call it 'an act of God' and our immediate response is one of sympathy and a sincere desire to help in the relief work.

As we learn more about what happened, we discover that not only was the drought predictable (the average rainfall had been recorded as decreasing over recent years and had to fall about last year to a critical level where crops would be unable to support men and beasts) but also that, in spite of the desert growing southwards each year, there is ample water available below the surface if the means are found to pump it up. (This is possible, even without using oil, because sun pumps do exist supplying whole villages with the water they need.) So the act of God looks a little like the distraction of man.

74

Then we probe a little deeper and discover that there are four major crops in the Sahel: ground-nuts, cotton, sorghum and millet. Of the first of these there are now 1200 different varieties (imagine, 1200 different sorts of peanut!) and these have been developed largely to produce drought resistant varieties. Of the second, cotton, production in the last ten years has gone up anywhere between four and ten times, depending on the country.

On the other hand the production of sorghum and millet which are the staple diets of 80% of the population has risen slower in the last ten years than the increase of population.

Why the disparity? Because the first two are for export and of concern to the Western world, the last two are merely the livelihood of the people. Vast amounts of investment, of technological skill, of irrigation, of research have been applied to the former, and none to the latter.

So not only does the act of God turn out to be an act of man, not only does our response of charity grow into a concern about justice (for love is not merely wishing a person well but seeking his good effectively, and thus incorporates a demand for effective justice if it is to be love at all), but also a problem that began as one about *them* is seen to be one about *us*. We are involved because of who we are and how we live.

I give that as a single clearly defined example of the general endemic injustice at work, not only between rich countries and poor, but within each country between those who have taken off and those who have not.

The main text of our culture, involved so closely as it is with economic processes, is written by and for those already in the main text, and because of the processes at work, those in the margin are kept there.

My present task is not to go into the economic and other forces which give rise to this innate violence, but rather to see how to seek truth as we discover our own involvement in them. We saw that an issue about *them* turns out to be an issue about *us*. In the end the only real question we have to ask is: who am I? What does it mean to be *me?*

What then does it mean to be white, middle-class, anglo-saxon, male, a monk (in my case; and in yours what?). These are what I find I am; they are invitations neither to guilt nor to pride, but to face what it means to be these things within the context of the social whole.

The question 'who am I?' is not primarily an introspective one, but one that seeks the truth of all those factors which make me who I am, both my own personality and also my relationship within the social whole (though that distinction between private and public self knowledge is less real than it sounds). It is the latter aspect of self knowledge that I am concerned with here. So let's start by looking at some of the illusions within our mental luggage which prevent us seeing rightly and, therefore, loving rightly.

In my experience illusions sometimes clear slowly, like mist on a frosty morning, but more often they clear quite suddenly, like removing sun-glasses. Their clearance is a moment of truth in life, the sudden 'a-ha' response which brings into clarity whole realms of understanding which were previously confused and inchoate.

This is the illusion that as long as those well established in the main text of our culture do better and better, pursuing their aims and growth-economics with vigour and enterprise sooner or later it is bound to trickle through to those in the margins. It is a special illusion in that it also has an economic theory to go with it.

People say for instance that just as we in this country went through an industrial revolution and took off as a result, so it is only a matter of time and Brazil, India, Tanzania, will pass through the same processes and get on the same band wagon.

In fact the causes for our own take off, including ample supplies of cheap raw materials, ample cheap labour (overseas and at home), and ready markets for our manufactured goods, show up the absolute impossibility of the whole world doing the same. The main text not only produces the margins as part of its being written, but needs the margins for its very existence.

In our society, based on consumption, it is necessary not only to supply but encourage consumers. This is why advertising has such an integral place in the writing of the main text. Potential consumers are those who already have the appetite, and it is to these that are addressed the constant pressure to have more, to have two where one has done, to have colour where black and white has done, to have variety where simplicity has done, to have mobility where stability has done, and such idolising of growth sets up the social norms which make people feel they belong. To be a family at home in our society is presented as being like unto the families of T.V. commercials. That is the norm, and its presentation creates inadequacy and alienation in the many who are in the margin, as well as creating the debilitating concern with 'having' and 'succeeding' which obsesses those in the main text.

In the example given of the Sahel disaster it is very clear how research and development has fed the already fed-up, and by distracting concern from *people*, effectively starved those in the margins.

This is broadly the process at work not only in international relations, and within our affluent nations, but also within many poorer nations, where the emergence of wealthy and power elites is one of the saddest aftermaths of their independence.

If we wish to clear our minds and hearts of the trickle through illusion, we need to take realistically the scriptural bias of love for the 'poor'. God's ways are not man's ways, and he happens to show more concern for those in the margins than those in the main text — unless these latter are willing to join him in such a concern for the dispossessed, the forgotten, the marginalised.

THE POOR-ARE-ALWAYS-WITH-YOU

'Don't get excited. Things today are basically no different than they have always been. Hunger and poverty are part and parcel of history. Of course we must do what we can to help, but you won't change things'.

And the illusion is doubly dangerous by borrowing a quotation from Christ himself (albeit out of context). The slightest knowledge of disasters such as the Sahel, cited above, reveals how wrong is this comfortable illusion that poverty *happens,* and is not *caused,* but in my experience the more and more acquainted one becomes with any form of marginalisation the more one is aware that poverty is created by the very same processes which set up the affluent. 10,000 families in this country are in substandard housing conditions, or have no house at all, not because we cannot build homes, nor because they are irresponsible, but because the pursuits of those of us in the main text create expectations and speculations, which inevitably create the margin without ability, without power. We are all involved because of who we are, and the options open to us are either to live off the system, (saying to ourselves 'surely God will not see', as the Psalmist puts it), or to become aware and work to free it of polarising tendencies.

By 'the poor', what do we mean? If our categories are merely those of wealth, so that the poor are those without money, then our only desire is to make the urban poor in this country into comfy middle-class property owners, to make the 'developing' (note the word) countries, good Western capitalists. No, what we are talking about is something much deeper; the poor are the dispossessed, the voiceless, those who because of their condition have no part to play in shaping their own history. The poor-are-always-with-you illusion is clung to for our own peace of mind, because to recognize that there are *causes* behind the conditions of those in the margin, is also to recognize that our vocation is not welfarism, hand-outs, foreign aid, but to so identify with the dispossessed as to be able to welcome and encourage them to have power, that is to take hold of their own decisions.

But that is bound to upset us, especially as we have a slight suspicion that in doing so they will catch from us, or find within themselves the same desire for power and profit of which we, too late, have come to repent. One thing seems clear to me now, that to be faithful we must get over our desire to help people and learn the great art of loving-by-identifying. This is the message for us of Christ's incarnation, his clear and deliberate identification with powerlessness which was the only way in which ultimate values and truth could be proclaimed.

It is not an optional part of Christian faith, but an essential part, that a person must identify with the 'least of my brethren', the forgotten, the dispossessed, the trapped, the powerless. This identification will take different forms. In the first place it depends upon a person's awareness of the processes at the root of injustice (different for one who sees the basic problem as being the accident of some having less than others, than for one who sees the assumed styles of life of the powerful as itself the basic problem). In the second place it depends on a person's situation in life: for one it can be a call to work immediately among the forgotten or oppressed, for another a refusal to work systems which are seen as unjust with no reasonable hope of changing, for another to be a voice for the voiceless in the houses and work of those who have the voice and power to shape society.

I remember before the Roman Synod (1971) on Justice a bishop said to me 'remember that one Mother Teresa is worth 1,000 Synods'. I think he is wrong, if the Synod could truly be a voice for the voiceless in the lives of those who tend not to hear. In many ways it is easier to go and work in Peru than to speak and live truth at home, for all authentic love-identification with the forgotten (whether overseas or in our midst at home) makes a man a stranger among his own. His hope is forced to be in God and with those 'friends', of whom Jesus spoke, who would not be known until the kingdom is fulfilled.

There is, of course, a sense in which 'the-poor-are-always-with-us', (apart from the special reference Christ's words had in their context), in that the social processes which polarise men into those with power and those without are the results not of some new situation but of the pride and blindness of the fallen human heart. Men are probably no more greedy today than they have been in previous ages.

However there are factors today which show up 'the-poor-are-always-with-you' as a bourgeois illusion today in a way that it would not have been in earlier times. I think these factors are:

1. That because of technology those who have power and resources today have far greater means at their disposal than ever in the past.

2. That because of the social sciences we now have means of analyzing the processes at work, and therefore the means of not only patching up the results but getting at the causes.

3. That because of modern communications and mass media, everyone knows about each other; those in the margin are aware of those who are not, and know that life need not be as it is. This is quite different from merely being in a marginal culture aware only of its own life and its own horizons.

4. That because our world is a village and its population more interdependent than ever before, the scale of those affected by unjust structures is far greater than before.

81

F

The poor-are-always-with-us is illusory not because, literally, it is untrue, but because it is an expression of an attitude which looks at destitution and suffering as the-way-things-are, somehow built into the universe by God, rather than the-way-things-need-not-be. They are seen not as caused, and therefore involving us all, but as happenings.

But that illusion is not as blind as the attitude, castigated constantly by Jesus, that anyone finding himself in the main text is there because of industrious and virtuous living, while anyone in the margin must be there because he is dissolute. 'Father' a lady assured me 'there is no poverty today, only mismanagement'.

One morning, two social workers discussed a film on T.V. about a desperate family whose son had got into ever worse problems. Said the first 'the wife's fingers were covered in nicotine; perhaps if they smoked less, they would have saved enough to help the boy'. Said the second 'you could only notice that because you are well enough established to have colour T.V.; and how do you know that she does not smoke as a result of the inevitable tensions in which they live?'

Which was cause and which effect? As the eye sees so is the problem.

'NICE'-PEOPLE-MUST-BE-'JUST'-PEOPLE

. . . . or more fully: injustice is caused by nasty people, but we are nice people, so we are not unjust.

How often has one heard, in discussions on our colonial past and present, people say 'you can't say that the system did the harm you say it did because my grandfather went out to India and he had the highest and most generous of intentions. That generation was a noble and generous one'.

Equally you find among the more naive lefties the basic assumption that every capitalist, every stock broker, every man in top management, is an ogre in disguise grinding the faces of the poor.

Each of these miss the real nature of justice and injustice.

If a trading and investment agreement between a firm in Europe and ground-nut growers in the Sahel in effect works to fill the pockets of a few producers, an élite, and distracts attention from the peasant people, excluding them from any real participation, then to say that an agreement works injustice is to say that the *agreement,* or the *economic structure* of which it is a part, is unjust. It is not in *the first instance* a value judgment on those involved in such a structure. People of the highest motivations are involved by the fact of where they are, not by virtue of any malice. We all are.

Any value judgment on the persons involved should not be directed at the fact of their involvement, but at whether or not they have reasonable means of being aware of such involvement, and whether, being aware, they really work to create justice or, if needs be, get out.

By and large our western idea of sin is very moralistic, that is it concentrates on moral failure, malice, laziness, being naughty etc., and tends to ignore intellectual failure, lack of insight, foolishness, blindness and so on. The eastern tradition is still like that of the earlier western tradition, in which the root of sin lies in ignorance and our real need is to overcome our blindness by enlightenment, by learning to see rightly, rather than the contemporary western emphasis on trying harder to behave better.

One of the tasks of faith is to illuminate what is going on, to open up the reality of situations and processes. And this is never an easy, painless or popular enlightening because our very involvement and vested interest in the structures we build, lead to great self-deception and illusion.

But the first question must always be: 'What is taking place?' and not 'Whose fault is it, who can we blame?'

IT-CAN'T-HAPPEN-TO-US

In July 1973 I listened to a talk by Dr E.F. Schumacher about oil and power supplies. 'What were we going to do when the lights went out? When the Arabs decided that their future lay in leaving underground the limited oil supplies which the world was so fast and increasingly using up? Men always had the option: be wise in time or face the chaos too late'. I remember being captivated by his presentation, but with that mental detachment, that inner smile, with which people must have listened to the prophets or read St John's Revelation. And then two months later it all started and he was vindicated. What is it in us that goes on saying: It can't happen to us, there is something quite special about our age and our situation which will guarantee the future?

In two years since then, the whole atmosphere has clouded over and people, rather lost and afraid, feel that time is running out. This sense of being lost, not knowing what or who can offer a pointer to the future, is the inevitable result of being lulled by the sense of well-being, of it-will-go-on-like-this-forever, which preceded it. The clear evidence of history is that when things go well a moral lassitude sets in, which is itself the climate in which dissolution sets in. Instead of being masters of their systems, men become enslaved by them, precisely because they deliver them the goods.

This was very much the situation in which Jesus found the established ideology of his time. 'We have a system of Law which can deliver the goods, can make men what they ought to be, can demand allegiance and secure the future'. It is not easy for us, looking with hindsight, to catch the outspoken and seemingly absurd quality of his confrontation with this settled ideology. A great and beautiful temple which had absorbed thousands of pounds and many decades of work, there before his eyes: the guarantor of God's abiding presence and the security of life. You see all this, it will all be razed, not a stone on a stone. For God must dwell in his people, not in houses made of stone nor in any system of law. The Sabbath was made for man not man for the Sabbath.

Always it is the same, we look for our security and well-being as guaranteed not by authentic hope, but by expectations that our system will deliver the goods. It is precisely because we do this that the system rigidifies, becomes master and not servant, distracts us from life and becomes its own downfall. Not surprising then that the downfall occurs when least expected (which is why the prophets were laughed at). It comes like a thief in the night, invited by the very fact that the householder is fast asleep in bed.

The vocation of Christ's messengers is not to hand on a ready-made complete kit of salvation, but constantly to interpret people's experience in the light of the kingdom. To do this today, in the West, and certainly for many people in this country, we need to show how anxiety and lostness can be interpreted and appropriated into oneself. It thereby becomes authentic *suffering*. To suffer, to sub-ferre, is to under pin, under bear, support. It is by thus appropriating what starts as external fear, that we turn what would be destructive and death dealing into some-thing creative and life giving. We learn that when expecta-tions dwindle hope can be born, not a naive wishful-thinking but a rediscovery of God's presence within times of trial and disintegration.

Last autumn, during the Synod of Bishops on Evangelization, it was suggested to Bishop Lamont of Rhodesia, that everything looked very black and hopeless for his people. He replied that quite the contrary was true and quoted, by heart, this passage from Christopher Fry's 'A Sleep of Prisoners':

The human heart can go to the lengths of God.
Dark and cold we may be, but this is no winter now.
The frozen misery of centuries breaks, cracks,
beings to move;
The thunder is the thunder of the floes,
The thaw, the flood, the upstart Spring.
Thank God our time is now when wrong comes up
to face us everywhere,
Never to leave us till we take the longest stride of
soul men ever took.
Affairs are now soul size.
The enterprise is exploration into God.

As we drove to the station after the meeting, the young
Oxfam staff member said that he always felt uneasy when
he heard Christians speak about suffering. No doubt he
himself was misled by a contemporary sort of welfare
thinking that life can be divided into two clear parts, the
negative — suffering, pain, destitution, death — and the
positive — joy, well-being, life, fulfilment; the former being
simply meaningless, the latter being simply good. But his
comment also pointed to a failure among Christians, who
often come to terms with much suffering in a way never
intended by Christ. Through a servile spirituality and a
domesticated reading of the Gospel we have applied the
invitation to take up the cross to every sort of suffering,
and talk of the will of God as if he really wanted suffering
and death.

It is important that we distinguish two forms of suffering, even if they are easier to distinguish on paper than in
real life. The first is what we suffer for the sake of truth
and love, the cost of discipleship, the second is what we
suffer because of infidelity.

When Christ asks us to take up our cross each day and
follow him he is referring to the first of these. For him the
'cross' refers to the rejection, the misunderstanding, the
conflicts and divisions, the loss of good friends, which are
inevitably incurred, indeed invited, by anyone who really
gives himself to the pursuit of truth and authentic love,
and by the Christian who seeks first the kingdom. He is
saying to those who want to follow him: seek the kingdom
and expect trouble; you will be strangers in the world and
even among your own; but fear not, I am with you. These
sufferings are to be welcomed, to be 'freely accepted' like

Christ's own cross, not because we can then come to terms with them as meaningful (all suffering is experienced as meaningless), but because they are in the service of truth and because our staying power before the meaningless character of such rejection forms us into real instruments of change for the future.

This suffering is seen most vividly in those who suffer imprisonment or death for the kingdom but it is also the cross freely accepted by those in many walks of life who are ready to abandon their jobs and what is familiar and secure for the sake of what is true and just; those who see, speak and do truth, for its own sake, and for love of people, and leave their future open to God.

Once we see this limited area of suffering as that to which Christ refers as 'the cross' and the 'will of God' freely to be accepted, much of scripture takes on a new light. When Paul for instance seems to glorify in the hardships he has undergone he is really glorifying in them as a measure of the good news of truth and love and the kingdom really coming over. Again when Matthew (ch. 25) recounts the parable of the Son of Man at the end of time calling the sheep into open pastures and leaving the goats behind, he is not saying, I think, that every man in prison, naked, homeless, is to be served as Christ (although that is true). Rather he is saying that if his apostles are true to faith and the kingdom they will, like himself, find themselves in prison, naked, homeless... And that those who serve them, precisely because they are suffering for the kingdom and are 'his brethren', are in fact acknowledging him in acknowledging them. ('My brethren' always refers to those called and sent in Christ's name; see Mt 10:42 and 18:1-5.)

The good news of God's liberating work among men involves suffering and its demands of truth and authentic love are divisive. We blunten the cutting edge of the Gospel if our longing to get on with people or our shyness make us over cautious of conflict. As the Peruvian theologian, Gutierrez, put it: the command was not to have no enemies, but to love our enemies, and we cannot love them if we do not have them.

*   *   *

But we also blunten the Gospel if we apply 'the cross' to that other form of suffering. The chaos of our personalities, the problem of a difficult uncle or spouse, the widespread social injustice we experience or identify with, our endless worries over our excessively complex life — these are not the 'will of God', 'our cross', but are for healing rather than accepting. They are for us to locate causes and free ourselves and others. Of course there is a sense in which such suffering has to be accepted first if we are to be able to open up the future; of course we have to appropriate into ourselves these areas in which we are tempted to play the innocent victim game, finding anyone but ourselves to blame. But we should not call such things the will of God as if he wants such death dealing forces for themselves.

When the prophets were tempted to feel sorry for themselves, God would say: stand up son of man, I want to talk to you. And to the apostles, when similarly tempted to feel incompetent, Christ would say: you men of little faith, fear not. He would not say: there, there, this is your cross.

Many of our anxieties and worries come from institutionalized blindness, as did that of the Pharisees. In the story of the blind man, John (ch. 9) draws a sharp contrast between Christ's determination to give sight to the man who recognized his blindness and Christ's inability to cure the unrecognized blindness of the Pharisees. The initial healing, a symbol and pledge of something much fuller, led the man on to delightful courage in the face of authoritarian intrigue, and also to humility and real vision when Christ searched him out. But the institutionalised blindness of the Pharisees, having twisted their eyes at every turn from being able to appreciate at all what was going on, brought out Christ's sharp rejoinder: If you were blind (and aware of your need) you would not be guilty, but since you are sure you see, your guilt, and blindness, remain. All of us have vested interests, unless we are the dispossessed of God, and it is these interests which create for us an endless succession of preoccupying problems, each solution turning into the next problem. The fears and anxieties created by such a process can hardly be called 'our cross'. Nor can we expect God to be too concerned about solving problems which our own infidelity and persistent idolatries have set us. What he calls us to is to come out into a new vision of things, a new land which he alone can show us. Faith moves most mountains not with bulldozers but by showing them up as pseudo.

* * *

Last year a young man who was a salesman for his firm came to our monastery to discuss holding courses there for Christians involved in business. He tried to argue that if we could show that being a good Christian would in fact make people more efficient then we could get grants from the various firms involved. He explained how he used to pray before each attempt at selling his product and how this made him more successful.

I ventured that it could possibly work out otherwise and that getting to know God in the Gospel sense might lead a person to failure rather than success. After all it led his own Son to the cross and we can hardly dissociate ourselves.

We went on to talk about other things.

We have today these two standards in contemporary spirituality: One says: all suffering is good, accept your cross. The other says: success is of God, he helps those who help themselves. These two can in fact dwell unresolved in each of us, but there are times when groups of people are formed spiritually by one or the other. It is my suspicion that the Catholic-Protestant divide in Northern Ireland springs from their spiritualities, the former having had an excessively servile-acceptance approach, preached in Catholic piety, and the latter a success oriented approach, preached in Calvinism.

Each of these is a simplistic understanding of the central mystery of our human condition, caught as we are within evil and suffering and yet totally dependent on a God who is wholly good and all powerful.

If he is really good, then he has obviously lost control and is not all powerful. Look at the massive injustice, evil and suffering in the world.

Well there is probably no answer to this. Of course we can come to see that many acute sufferings and disasters arise less as happenings (and therefore called 'acts of God'!)

and far more as the results of human infidelity — men refusing to concentrate their minds and hearts and skills on what really matters. And of course we can also come to see and experience, that many people grow to greatness in suffering, touching depths of human reality and generosity which we are normally unaware of because of well-being and activity. This was beautifully caught in a letter of Teilhard de Chardin to his sister lying seriously ill in her convent:

> O Marguerite, my sister, while I, in dedication to the positive forces of the Universe, was traversing continents and oceans passionately absorbed in watching all the tints of the earth take on a fuller colour, you, motionless, laid low by sickness, were silently, in the deepest depths of your self, converting into light the darkest shadows of the world. Which of us, tell me, as the Creator looks down on us, will he say has chosen the better part?
>
> (Quoted in '*The Faith of Teilhard*' by de Lubac)

But whatever the glimpses we have that suffering is not simply bad, and well-being is not simply good, we are still confronted by the profoundly meaningless character of evil, of suffering, of death. Our deep longing to interpret these realities of our world is never answered. The humanist in each of us can only be confronted by these as problems and our very busyness in trying to solve them only makes more acute the meaningless character of this dark side of human existence. The Christian in each of us does not find a solution, but does shift the problem into a mystery, the cross through which and not around which God raises to life.

It is always noticeable at meetings on various social matters that the faces of those who know suffering, in themselves or those they serve, show forth a joy and peace in clear contrast to the faces of those who are only anxious spectators with a vicarious involvement. Perhaps this inner peace and joy come from glimpsing a little of the great mystery of which Julian of Norwich spoke:

Our Lord said to me once, 'All things shall be well'. Another time he said, 'You shall see yourself that all manner of things shall be well' and in these two statements 1 understood various things.

One, is that he wants us to know that he takes care not only of big things, but also of little things too. This is what he means when he says, '*All* manner of things shall be well'. He wants us to know that not even the tiniest matter will be forgotten.

Another insight is this: there is so much injustice that we know about, and such unhappiness suffered, that it can seem impossible to us that it will ever end. If we experience this, feeling unhappy and depressed, we cannot calmly wait on God as we ought. The reason for this is that our minds are unenlightened — too limited and too simple — so that we cannot grasp the profound wisdom, might and goodness of the blessed Trinity. This is what our Lord means when he says, 'You shall see for *yourself* that all manner of things shall be well'. It is as if he had said, 'If you believe trustingly now, in the end you will see everything fulfilled, and be overjoyed yourself as well'.

I find real encouragement in these next five words: 'I can make everything well'. As I understand them, there is a 'Deed' which the blessed Trinity will carry out in time; but when this will be, or how it will be done, is unknown to all creation, and will remain unknown until it is accomplished.

He tells us this because he wants us to be more serene within ourselves, and more settled in our love: we must not get enmeshed in those things which hold us back from joyful awareness of him. This is the marvellous 'Deed' our Lord has planned from eternity, known only to himself and treasured deep in his heart. This is the way he makes all things well. Just as the blessed Trinity called creation from nothing, so shall that same Trinity transform all that is evil into good. . .

I thought it was impossible that 'all manner of things' should be well, as our Lord showed me. But I had no other answer to this revelation except this: 'That which is impossible for you is not impossible for me; I will stand by what I have said, in every circumstance, and I will make all things well'.

Thus was I taught, by God's grace, that I ought to cling steadfastly to the faith as I understood it, and I should really believe all things shall be well, as our Lord showed me. . . How it shall be done is unknown among creatures, nor shall it be known until it is accomplished; at least, that is how I understood our Lord's meaning at the time.

(*Revelations of Divine Love,* chapter 32)

WHAT'S-MINE-IS-MINE-I-EARNED-IT-DIDN'T-I?

This is perhaps the deepest of all illusions, because the subconscious assumptions we make about what it means to own or to earn are at the basis of most decisions and interpreations of life. What does it mean to own the Bic biro which is writing this, or the clothes you are wearing, or your house, or the oil under the North Sea? Very few people ever ask those questions and ours is an age which has no articulate philosophy of ownership. It does have strong unquestioned presuppositions. For instance we penalise heavily any crime of theft and our prisons are full of men who have offended against property. But we have no system for penalising those who hoard or spend their life allowing ever more to gather in around them. But in the last analysis it will be the latter who are seen to work the greater injustice.

One measure of our illusory attitude to ownership is the way in which we misinterpret or listen through muffled ears to Christ's teachings. When we read, for instance, his story of Dives and Lazarus we take it for granted that he was only criticising a rich man for not giving alms to a poor man, alms or welfare handouts or foreign aid. But in fact he was there addressing the Pharisees (who were by the way not the horrible ogres we sometimes suppose them to have been, but mostly very sincere, good people). He was recalling to their attention their own rabbinic tradition that all things are not only given by God but belong to him. This being especially true of land, and anyone who 'owns' land, or indeed a house or farm on it, is not a simple freeholder, but is a tenant-of-God. That tenancy requires that part of what is 'earned', part of the fruits of one's tenancy, belongs to God. A tithe is due. But how do you pay God? Well you pay him in his poor, the *anawim* of Yahweh. So Dives was withholding from Lazarus what was his due as well as failing in charity.

Christ was also warning that the issue at stake is an ultimate one, to do with life or death, being set free or being trapped. What traps the poor is not poverty itself, but the circle of poverty, and what traps the rich is not riches or power but the circle of riches and power. One thing leading endlessly to another. Christ is saying that what breaks the vicious circle for Dives, which in the end is more death-dealing than that of Lazarus, breaks also the circle of poverty of Lazarus. Liberation from the two circles is by means of understanding the inter-relation of the two circles.

*   *   *

In my experience a person's awareness and vision takes a definitive step forward when he stops thinking in terms of giving of some of his surplus to charities and he starts to tithe his income. By so doing he recognizes that his own situation as such involves him, rather than his being an innocent spectator who can pick and choose out of the generosity of his heart what to do with what is 'his'. His gift becomes a truly sacramental sign. It would be excellent if the churches encouraged people to tithe (and of course did so with church finances as well) rather than endlessly having collections for charities. A tithe can be set at 1%, 5%, 10%, 30%, but always rather above the level where its effect is not felt.

There is of course a danger that such tithing can become rather mean and not liberating, a sort of parcelled out business deal. There is the further step in which a man no longer parcels out, but reaches a spiritual freedom in seeing all things so really as gifts-and-so-for-sharing that he spontaneously and joyously simply gives. This is the outflowing of a very basic attitude to things.

'Men ought to possess external things not as their own, but as common, in such a way, that is, that they are ready to communicate them.' 'Those things which some possess in excess of reasonable needs are owed by natural law to the sustenance of the poor.'

(Thomas Aquinas, *S.T.* II II 66 art 2 & 7)

* * *

What a man earns or owns is far more a function of the whole social fabric in which he works and lives, than a simple measure of his own hard work and contribution. This is equally true for more precious resources in his life than material wealth; it is especially true for instance of education, perhaps the greatest of all a person's resources. But in every case we find a sharp contrast between the illusory view of the world which sees all our resources as well-earned achievements to be prized, and the light of faith which shows up all as gift and communal. This immediately turns inside out most of our assumptions about how to use these resources. Instead of turning them in on themselves, so that wealth creates wealth, power creates power, they are turned outwards in loving service; gifts are for sharing, with a special eye on the most forgotten. The way we use gifts is the way we glorify or blaspheme the Giver.

But there is never any hint in the gospels that power, property or pleasure are in themselves evil, and a truly Christian response to finding oneself with these things at one's disposal is never a sense of guilt or self-hatred. It is

97

easy for a puritan ethic linked with middle-class worry to make people feel awful about being who they are. But nothing in life is in itself bad and there is nothing wrong in power or wealth in themselves; it is just that they have a strong tendency to make people blind and small-worldly.

There is an amazing comment by Christ in Luke 16 where he has been speaking of us being stewards of God's gifts and therefore not owners in our own right. He goes on to ask: 'If you cannot be trusted with what is not yours (things external to one's real self), who will give you what is your very own (life, peace, joy, God himself)?'

Christ's invitation is always to spiritual freedom and maturity. Christian poverty, as a virtue, always springs from a desire to be free to follow Christ. The strange paradox is that when we are possessed by nothing, then we are truly ourselves and also the whole world is ours. And this is just as true of our local communities or families, and our large scale social organizations, as it is for us as individuals (though immensely harder to work out in practice). To use resources in the spirit of given-and-so-for-sharing is both for the liberation of those who find themselves possessors as it is for the dispossessed. And it is the only road which Christian faith offers us if we seek to be free to 'know God' in our concrete circumstances.

*　　*　　*

Needless to say that this is light years away from the standard what's-mine-is-mine illusion of our age. Often when such matters of Christian poverty are discussed an immediate reaction is set up: but what's wrong with having things? and if there's nothing wrong then stop binding on.

But life is not made up of what is wrong, and therefore to be shunned, and what is right, and therefore to be enjoyed without limit. It is because we tend to think that way today, that our society has no assumed ascesis or discipline in our use of good things, no accepted limits, no sense of enough-is-enough, no sense that indulgence in good things destroys spiritual awareness and perception.

In the parable of the wedding feast, the invitations went out first to those who, far from being occupied in wrong-doing, 'sin' in the accepted sense, were occupied in perfectly innocent occupations: one had got married and was on honeymoon, one had bought a house and was decorating, one had bought a car which needed running-in. They were preoccupied in good things and that was why they never recognized the invitation for what it was. It is what preoccupies the head and the heart which prevents people seeing rightly and for most of us today it is just because we have so many good things to enjoy, so many schemes to attend to, so much business to complete, that we cannot see reality nor read the signs of the times; we fail to find life, being preoccupied with life substitutes. 'Ah! If you in your day had only understood the message of peace; but alas, it is hidden from your eyes.' To recognize the message of peace, to know the presence and the will of God in our actual situation is never to be had just for the asking. We cannot expect to lead any way of life, pursue any ends, and yet somehow expect to come to see the will of God. Christ was quite clear that whether or not a man, a community or a society, is to be able to recognize truth, recognize the reign of God in the actual world, and open out the future in hope, depends upon where its practical preoccupations are centred. Decisions about lifestyle and practical pursuits are prerequisites and not merely the results of seeing rightly. Neither praxis nor theory, practical life nor perceptive reflection, are possible except in dialogue with the other.

'Do not model yourselves on the behaviour of the world around you, but let your behaviour change, modelled by your new mind. This is the only way to discover the will of God and know what is good, what it is that God wants, what is the perfect thing to do' (Romans 12).

There is today an increasing discussion about lifestyle; cutting down, or out, meat, driving at under 50 m.p.h., travelling by public transport, refusing to buy over-packed, over-publicised or over-processed goods, recycling waste. These can be done a) to help solve our social problems, b) to save money to share with those in need, c) as a symbolic purpose of intent to enable us to bring pressure on government and other bodies. But however good these motivations may be, I think the really faith-centred motivations must be: d) to act as permanent reminders and symbols to ourselves of our identification with the poor and dispossessed (only realistic if such lifestyle discipline goes further than clever playing about), e) to be a way of seeking to use all things in a loving and non-violent relation with nature and with all men, f) to free our minds and hearts to grow in perception and to know the reign of God in concrete reality.

Be still, and know what it means for me to be God.

FROM AFRICA

To us in Africa land was always recognized as belonging to the community. Each individual within our society had a right to the use of land, because otherwise he could not earn his living and one cannot have the right to life without also having the right to some means of maintaining life. But the African's right to land was simply the right to use it; he had no other right to it, nor did it occur to him to try to claim one.

The foreigner introduced a completely different concept — the concept of land as a marketable commodity. According to this system, a person could claim a piece of land as his own private property whether he intended to use it or not. I could take a few square miles of land, call them 'mine', and then go off to the moon. All I had to do to gain a living from 'my' land was to charge a rent to the people who wanted to use it. If this piece of land was in an urban area I had no need to develop it at all; I could leave it to the fools who were prepared to develop all the other pieces of land surrounding 'my' piece, and in doing so automatically to raise the market value of mine. Then I could come down from the moon and demand that these fools pay me through their noses for the high value of 'my' land — a value which they themselves created for me while I was enjoying myself on the moon! Such a system is not only foreign to us, it is completely wrong.

(Julius Nyerere, President of Tanzania)

FROM INDIA

With God's help I can enter every heart. If I can be the agent of both the rich and the poor I shall be glad. For the poor I am striving to win rights. For the rich I am striving to win moral development. If one grows materially and the other spiritually, who then is the loser? Besides, what is land? How is it possible for anyone to consider himself the 'owner' of it? Like air and water, land belongs to God. To claim it for oneself is to oppose the very will of God. And who can be happy if they oppose his will?

(Vinoba Bhave)

101

FROM NICARAGUA

In respect of riches, then, just or unjust
of goods be they ill-gotten or well-gotten:
                    All riches are unjust
All goods,
            ill-gotten.
If not by you, by others.
Your title-deeds may be in order. But
did you buy your land from its true owner?
And he from its true owner? And the latter ... ? etc.
Though your title go back to the grant of a king
                    was
the land ever the king's?
Has no one ever been deprived of it?
And the money you receive legitimately now
from client or Bank or National Funds
                    or from the U.S. Treasury
was it never ill-gotten? Yet
do not think that in the perfect Communist State
Christ's parables will have lost relevance
nor St Luke 16, 9 have lost validity
                    and riches be no longer UNJUST
nor that you will no longer have a duty to distribute them!

                    (Ernesto Cardenal, Cistercian monk)

(Use money, tainted as it is, to win you friends and thus make
sure that when it fails you, they will welcome you into the tents
of eternity... If you cannot be trusted with what is not yours,
who will give you what is your very own? ... (Some) who loved
money, heard all this and laughed at him. — Luke 16)

TO THE GREAT CHIEF IN WASHINGTON

How can you buy or sell the sky — the warmth of the land?
The idea is strange to us. Yet we do not own the freshness of
the air or the sparkle of the water. How can you buy them for us?
We will decide in our time.

102

Every part of the earth is sacred to my people.
Every shining pine needle, every sandy shore, every mist of
  the divine woods,
every clearing and humming insect is holy in the memory of
  my people.
We know that the white man does not understand our ways.
One portion of the land is the same to him as the next,
for he is a stranger who comes in the night and takes from
  the land whatever he needs.
The earth is not his brother, but his enemy,
and when he has conquered it he moves on.
He leaves his fathers' graves behind and he does not care.
He kidnaps the earth from his children. He does not care.
His fathers' graves and his children's birthright are forgotten.
His appetite will devour the earth and leave behind only a desert.
The sight of your cities pains the eyes of the redman.
But perhaps it is because the redman is a savage and does not
  understand. . .

One thing we know that the white man may one day discover.
Our God is the same God.
You may think now that you own him as you wish to own
  our land.
But you cannot. He is the God of man.
And his compassion is equal for the redman and the white.
The earth is precious to him,
and to harm the earth is to heap contempt on its creator.
The whites too shall pass — perhaps sooner than other tribes.
Continue to contaminate your bed, and you will one night
  suffocate in your own waste.
When the buffalo are all slaughtered, the wild horses all tamed. . .
where is the thicket? Gone.
Where is the eagle? Gone.
And what is it to say goodbye to the swift pony and the hunt,
the end of living and the beginning of survival.
We might understand if we knew what it was that the white
  man dreams,
what hopes he describes to his children on long winter nights,
what visions he burns into their minds, so that they will wish
  for tomorrow.
But we are savages. The white man's dreams are hidden
  from us. . .

If we sell you our land, love it as we have loved it.
Care for it as we have cared for it.
Hold in your mind the memory of the land, as it is when
you take it.
And with all your strength, with all your might, and with
all your heart —
preserve it for your children, and love it as God loves us all.
One thing we know — our God is the same God.
Even the white man cannot be exempt from the common destiny.

(from a letter from Chief Seattle of the Duvamish tribe
to the President of the United States in 1855)

LETTER TO A SEMINARIAN

Warrington
Nov '74

Dear Paul,

You asked me, as you served me a pint of beer at St Edward's club that night, what on earth so many priests were doing in a monastery when they could be saving souls as parish priests. You did not mean it polemically and I take it as a straight enquiry. I hope I have your question right.

In order to answer your question, I think we need a broader understanding of what we are involved in. We are not primarily concerned with converting individuals, but with the kingdom. So let's have a look at what Christ meant by the kingdom.

We have made mistakes in the past either by supposing that it meant *heaven,* the after-life, or that it means *the Church* as a well-defined society. Of course both of these are partly true, but if we say kingdom=heaven, then people despise all things material, sexual, political, and finish up alienated from the world in which God has actually put them; if we say kingdom=Church, then we see the Church as sharp edged, members inside with all the answers, non-members outside with all the problems, in bad faith, and left to some mysterious mercy of God quite different from what *we* know about.

God is at work at all times, in all places, and in every person. Christian faith is the living recognition of that, the interpretation of every part of life, the dark side as well as the light, the secular as well as the sacred, as coming within the scope of the active will of a loving Father, a personal God with whom we can discourse, struggle, be knocked down and raised up.

To enter 'the kingdom' is to live in full recognition of this intimate and all embracing dominion of God. This entry is not merely intellectual nor moral, it is a new creation within us because it is achieved in us by the work of God himself, a participation in his own inner life.

The Church is not the enclosure of those who are safe, but the sacrament, the clear (more or less clear) statement and sign of the otherwise hidden (more or less hidden) work of God in all people at all times. But she is sacrament in the sense of enhancing and effecting that work, not merely pointing it out.

If we see the Church as a sacrament, a sign, in this way, rather than an enclosure, then the role of religious is easier to understand. But rather than talk about religious in general I'll talk about monks because it's monastic life in which I'm involved and I think your question was really about that.

Many religious orders were founded with a special work or need in mind, such as teaching, nursing, or welfare. Their existence is not justified by that work as such because after all lay people can do such work, in some cases rather better. But by their religious consecration they show forth the work of education, of healing, of service, as God's work; they show it as part of the kingdom. Their prayer is supportive of their work, without prayer their work would lose its divine reference, but even so their prayer will fit into the demands of their work. So in general we can say that such orders exist for a purpose.

Monastic life on the other hand does not exist for any specific purpose, but for living out a total way of life. It is a carefully studied, articulated way of life in which each part is seen in direct reference to God, within his dominion, his kingdom. Monastic life is not defined by the particular work that monks do, even though that work is an integral part of its totality. If you like, monastic life is a total interpretation of life in which every element bears direct reference to God; it is the monk's vocation to live out in community that which the priest or missioner proclaims from the pulpit.

It will be worth quoting a few phrases from St Benedict to illustrate this sense of immediate reference to God in each part of life:

'The abbot' is 'believed to represent Christ'.
Buying and selling 'Let not avarice set in, but let goods be sold a little cheap . . . that in all things God may be glorified'.

Brethren 'The brethren shall obey one another, knowing that by this way will they go to God'.
The sick 'Before all and above all, care must be taken of the sick so that they are served as Christ himself. . . And let the sick on their part consider that they are being served for the honour of God. . .'

Guests 'Let all guests be received like Christ. . . In

greeting guests let the greatest humility be shown . . . and so let Christ be worshipped in them, for he is received in their persons. In receiving poor men, and pilgrims special attention should be shown, because in them is Christ most truly welcomed'.

But although each aspect of life is seen as God's work, above all else the daily prayer is 'the work of God', the *opus Dei*. And Benedict insists that nothing else should be allowed to take prior place. Prayer is not seen in the first place as a support work for the rest of life, but as an end in itself (though I think that distinction is less easy than it sounds). The structure of the various offices, both their placing within the day and their individual lengths and characters, are delicately worked out. It is the most difficult area for renewal on monastic life to get the balance between the hours of prayer and the rest of life right, when active work tends to press in on all sides.

* * *

From some of the things I have mentioned you will see that monastic life as such, is really a lay vocation rather than a clerical one, and it is low profile at that — it is non-enthusiastic, tends not to bear its faith on its shirt cuffs, and is very much geared to ordinary people making a reasonably good job of directing their whole life to God.

In fact the monks, though not the nuns, of the English Benedictines have, by their history, an amalgam of the monastic, priestly and educational vocations, and I expect that their life is nonetheless legitimate for that. Certainly such messy type monasticism provides a scope and purpose and basic sense which saves us from some of the special problems of men called to the monastic life *tout simple*.

But in answer to your question I focus on the monastic facet as such. Does it have a mission? Yes, but not 'mission' like the pulpit or overseas missionaries. To assess the mission of monasteries it is necessary to look at the evidence of history, or at the contemporary place of monasteries in the Church and society at large; what God uses a person or community for is not the same as what they are setting out to do. A loving and happy family in the parish here in Warrington has a profound influence on other families and on young people getting engaged; but if such a family set out to be such a witness it would destroy itself overnight in the process. So too a monastery is first and foremost consecrated to God, forgetful of its social mission, which it leaves to God as and how he chooses (though to be honest an awareness of that wider mission is a great stimulus to take seriously one's vocation).

A few months ago a young woman who had read history at Cambridge and done social work in housing in London came to see me — having decided at a time of deep spiritual disarray that it was for her a moment of truth — and I asked her first why she wanted to become a Catholic. 'Because I have found in your worship a sense of the mystery of faith which I have not found anywhere else.' And why did she want to join a religious community? 'Because everywhere else our world always does things for the sake of something else, everything is done to achieve something or to prove something. In a religious community I feel that each day will be for itself, life will be its own end.'

St Paul refers to us as God's work of art and if monastic life as a whole is God's work of art we can hope that what Coleridge said is true, 'A work of art must contain within itself the reason why it is so and not otherwise'.

Chuang Tse, an early disciple of Confucius, said:

The mountain tree asks to be cut down.
Fat added to the fire consumes itself.
The cinnamon tree is useful so it is slashed.
Everyone knows the usefulness of the useful,
but no one knows the usefulness of the useless.

*　　*　　*

I think, Paul, that all this adds up to the fact that our monastic vocation only makes sense in terms of faith. If I mention one or two pointers as to how God seems to use the monastic presence in the Church and society at large, it is only to help you, and me, to see why God calls some people to this way of life.

By and large in this, our post Christian world, people arc bored by Christian language. With a yawn they say: please don't shove all those words at us, we've heard them all before. But they take their hand from their mouth and open their eyes as soon as they can see what *difference* it makes.

In your future walk of life as a priest, and in mine as a monk-cum-priest, what will really speak to people is not Christian truth but Christian truth-lived. I am sure that the real growth points for the Church are wherever people are getting together to discover new or ancient ways of changing their life under the light of truth. Monasteries are structured to enable this to happen in one particular way, though it demands a constant seeking for truth-requiring-to-be-lived which is our third Benedictine vow, *conversio morum.*

The world says: you need a career to be happy; we say (or should) we have no careers, but we are happy. The world says: consume more and more, you need to acquire things to be satisfied; we say (or should): we don't have more and more, and we are happy. The world says: God is a distraction from being really human; we say (or should): our life is God-centred and tell us, do you find us human or less than human? The world says: we can organize security for people; we say (or should): without a vision of man there is no security, with one it is unnecessary. And so on. The monastery should stand as a counter witness to the logic of the world, when that logic is the cleverness of men and not the foolishness of God.

When Thomas More wrote his Utopia he never put it out as a possible way of reorganizing society, and when people dismiss a thing as utopian, implying that it is just impractical day-dreaming, they miss More's point. His Utopians were meant to hold up a prophetic light to the men of his age, to challenge the various idolatries which were tearing society apart. In somewhat the same way, monasteries should hold out a prophetic challenge and encouragement to people to take seriously what man has always found it difficult to take seriously.

The three great idolatries of man are power, property and pleasure. Each of these in itself is a good thing (God save us all from Puritanism) for it is the nature of idols that they are in themselves good and God-given. But still we tend to idolise them, so it is no accident that the three classical religious vows correspond to these three idolatries.

Obedience, the emptying out of one's power, the love of powerlessness; *poverty,* the detachment from and sharing of property; *chastity,* the dedication of affections and pleasure to the one love behind and beyond all others. You can see that the practical living out of these in community should act as a Utopia for contemporary society. A sort of living hope to men who feel lost and alienated and bored in an idolatrous world that life can be other, that faith does overcome the world, and that lived-truth does set men free.

You know us, Paul, well enough to read such theorising with a certain questioning: does Thomas think that his monastery really provides such a prophetic sign of hope to our contemporary world? We ask the same question.

History is full of examples of men who are called by vocation to be marginal, slowly becoming (usually by their very success) part of the main text and no longer in the margin. Their inner light fades, their dynamism runs down, imagination becomes smothered by expediency. As Proverbs put it: the people die from lack of vision.

But in such situations it seems even more important to articulate the ideal, for the future is either death through suffocation, or renewed life in rediscovering the excited foolishness of the original monastic vision — although the practical implications of such renewal always causes pain and misunderstanding.

If we are entering a new dark age in our society at large the marginal, prophetic and utopian vocation of monasteries will become vital as signs of living hope. The times urge monks to be true to their inner calling.

*　　*　　*

There is also a prophetic aspect of monasteries to the

Church herself. Once our thinking moves away from seeing the Church as a well defined society to seeing her as sacrament of the kingdom, then we must be ready for surprises. The kingdom has a tendency to appear where and when not expected. When Christ spoke of the Spirit blowing where it chooses he knew from experience his own amazement at finding the kingdom bursting out in pagans (the Syrophoenician woman, the centurion and so on) and his own dismay at not finding it where it should have been evident (Nicodemus for instance). It seems likely that it was those moments which helped to evolve his own mission as messiah. But they are similarly experienced by many people today, in ecumenical work and in many other fields. We all need to learn that the Spirit is a joker.

It seems that monastic groups have a special role in saying 'yes' to where the kingdom appears in unexpected places, secular or non-Catholic, and saying 'no' to where it fails to appear in expected religious places. This has something to do with monastic life being a rather low profile Christian lifestyle which undercuts various accepted religious attachments. Be that as it may we all have to go through the rather painful discovery, if we are to be faithful to God, that 'the Church has many whom God has not; and God has many whom the Church has not' (St Augustine). Part of monks' service to the Church is thus to help her free herself from cultural religiosity and encourage ecumenism in its wide sense.

* * *

I think, Paul, to appreciate the monastic phenomenon in the Church is to appreciate the inner mystery of the Church and see beyond her merely as organization. We have largely lost in the West the really communal bond of all believers, the communion of saints, which the East appreciates so much better. What for instance do you make of this:

> 'All good done by the saints (in the broad non-hagiographic sense) is shared among all who abide in charity; whoever lives in charity has a part in all good that is done throughout the whole world.'
>
> (St Thomas Aquinas)

Perhaps the lone hermit is more an integral part of the Church, of us that is, than the activist Christian who, having lost the heart of faith, sets out to do more and more good.

*　　*　　*

I don't know if any of that really answers your question. I have had 18 years in a monastery and 1 year working in a parish. I think in many ways that your vocation as a priest is tougher than is the monk's living in community — at least as long as you seek the kingdom and don't settle for mediocrity.

Working on a parish one's life of prayer and study, and one's love of a modicum of poverty, require great self discipline. It has been humbling for me to discover how much of that discipline, which I had thought was in me, had in fact been shared as a result of the community's overall discipline. But then part of the point of community, in any form, is to enable us to do together what we can't do on our own. And I suspect that priests from now on must work to build and encourage supportive communties for prayer and work, unless they want to become mere lone social workers which is hardly their vocation.

Shalom,

Thomas.

FOR WHOM THE BELL TOLLS

Perchance he for whom this Bell tolls may be so ill
that he knows not it tolls for him;
and perchance I may think myself so much better than I am,
as that they who are about me, and see my state,
may have caused it to toll for me, and I know not that.
The Church is Catholic, Universal, so are all her actions;
all that she does belongs to all.
When she baptizes a child, that action concerns me;
for that child is thereby connected to that Head which is
    my Head too,
and engrafted into that body, whereof I am a member.
And when she buries a man, that action concerns me.
All mankind is of one Author, and is one volume;
when one man dies, one chapter is not torn out of the book,
but translated into a better language;
and every chapter must be so translated.
God employs several translators;
some pieces are translated by age, some by sickness, some by war,
    some by injustice;
but God's hand is in every translation,
and his hand shall bind up all our scattered leaves again,
for that Library where every book shall lie open one to another.
As therefore the Bell that rings to a sermon
calls not upon the preacher only, but upon the congregation
    to come,
so this Bell calls us all.
The Bell doth toll for him that thinks it does;
and though it intermit again,
yet from that minute that that occasion wrought upon him,
he is united to God...
Who bends not his ear to any bell, which upon any occasion rings?
But who can remove it from that bell, which is passing a piece
    of himself out of this world?

No Man is an Island entire of itself;
every Man is a piece of the Continent, a part of the Main;
if a clod be washed away by the sea, Europe is the less,

as well as if a promontory were, as well as if a manor of thy
friends were or of thy own;
any Man's death diminishes me, because I am involved
in Mankind;
and therefore never send to know for whom the Bell tolls;
it tolls for thee.

(John Donne, Devotions XVII)

COPING WITH BAFFLEMENT

(Written for Christian Aid, Dec. 1972)

For many, the journey to bafflement is in three stages. First we meet human suffering, poverty, hunger at a practical and immediate level. What is needed is food, clothing, medicines. This is first aid, it is fairly consoling to the giver, and it is external to his own life: a problem about 'them'.

Then we realize that it is better for the destitute to farm than be given food, to have education rather than cash, self-reliant development rather than outside aid. This is less consoling for the giver because the results are less obvious. It is rather less 'external' because it admits that 'they', the destitute, are the same sort of people as 'us'.

Then we arrive at the third stage. We discover the amazing extent to which our own Western world is geared to its own success, to gratify its own needs; and that the destitute world is held destitute, not by their failure to work and catch up, but by our own taken-for-granted living standards and economic growth. This discovery is not consoling at all. The issue has ceased to be about 'them' and is really now all about 'us'.

The immediate by-product of this level of awareness,

this sensitivity to the injustice built into the system that has nurtured us and which we take so much for granted — the immediate by-product is a blank sense of bafflement.

Bafflement in the 1970s has a number of special characteristics. Some are these:

— We live in immediate contact with every corner of the planet. On T.V., on radio, in newspapers, and in people we meet, we 'know' by immediate audio-visual contact the great distress and anguish of men. We want to take the whole world on our shoulders, not just the village. Or we switch off.

— If there were scapegoats to blame, we would not feel frustrated. In the past there have usually been scapegoats — the Germans, the Reds, the Blacks, the Wogs. But now it's us, the whole structural fabric of our competing and greedy society. We can't find a 'them' to pin it on.

— The vastness and intricate complexity of our system gives the impression of being beyond anyone's control. It will go on regardless, and we feel deeply alienated. We are relentlessly caught up in a system which is not in our own real interest, or in the true interest of mankind.

— We have been taught to accept the god of growth, that every graph must go up: living standards, wages, productivity, whatever. But now we all wonder if that was not a false idol. Can graphs go exponentially up for ever? Anyhow, do we like what we get?

— Time was when Christians had a clear world model. The 'world' was basically dangerous. God was safe and saving. So the world was expected to be evil. Then Marx had another clear world model: faith was phoney because it made out that 'real' man was other-worldly. Real man however was political, economic man. Man is what his world is. Change it, and you change him. Today we have no world model with which to interpret our bafflement. We need a model which takes the 'world' totally seriously precisely because its real value lies beyond its own immediate limitations; a model based both on the Incarnation and on the kingdom to come. But this is as yet absent from general Christian thinking, and without such a model we are baffled.

When a person is thoroughly baffled one of three things must happen. He may become apathetic, switch off, decide the whole thing is going too fast and get off while the going is good. He opts out, or — which comes to the same thing — settles for a comfortable little bourgeois world turned in on itself.

Secondly, he may become angry, not in a positive, creative sense, but in a negative, destructive sense. The sort of anger that looks dramatic and effective in the short run, but is fruitless in the long term.

Thirdly, he may take his bafflement, his sense of desperation, as a moment of truth, of reflection, of being open to a whole new way of seeing things. It is precisely the moment when man despairs of his own categories, his own solutions, his own assurance, that he is most open to the word of God. It turns out that his own categories were just too small, too petty, to be worthy of God or, for that matter, of man. But this option — of taking bafflement as a moment of truth — must involve suffering and patience and prayer, none of which are popular.

'We were so utterly crushed that we despaired of life itself. Why, we felt that we had received the sentence of death; but that was to make us rely not on ourselves but on God who raises the dead . . . on him we have set our hope that he will deliver us' (St Paul: 2 *Corinthians* 1, 8-10).

We turn to God to solve our problems, and we call this 'faith'. We turn to God to preserve us from trials and distress, and we call that 'faith'. But Jesus rebuked the apostles for that. They said, 'Lord, save us, we are sinking'. And he said, 'You men of little faith'. So much of our seeking God is really self-pity, and we have to be set free from that.

In bafflement we turn to God to sort things out in the way we want them. But instead, he invites us to come out into a new land, somewhere unfamiliar, risky. We have to listen, and learn, and be obedient (*ob audire*, to be a listener), in order to overcome our blindness. Faith is to discover that God's initiative has dominion in his world, and that God's ways are not our ways.

The apostles had hoped for a political messiah, a man who would solve problems. What they got was a creator who made fantastic demands on them, a messiah who sank himself in the depths of human distress and death, and called them, in their turn, to disgusting deaths — Stephen, Paul, Peter. Why? The world is God's, he has not lost control; life and joy and peace emerge from the very heart of distress and suffering and bafflement. Resurrection, salvation. Why? We do not know.

We do know, and Jesus made it quite clear, that to see things with the sensitive eyes of faith necessarily involves trials and pain — and above all the prolonged dis-ease of feeling a stranger in 'the world'. In the New Testament, faith is perseverance and staying power. It is not an 'act of faith' which can be made all at once. It is this above all that aligns the disciple to Christ. As John wrote to the early Christians, 'I share with you, in Jesus, the tribulation, and the kingdom, and the patient endurance' (*Revelation* 1:9).

Patient endurance: this was not the stoic putting-up-with-things because they were tough (and the bloodier the better). It was not our contemporary 'martyrdom to self-hood' (me over against everyone else). It was not resignation (there can be a false, masochistic, 'resignation to the will of God'). Nor was it evasion of the real issues (with the consoling thought that it's all too much for little me anyhow). No. Patient endurance was (and is) a uniquely Christian virtue. It is centred on Christian hope, which takes our present distress and puts it in the context of final triumph and joy. It enables us to accept without tiredness or apathy the long interval which separates our present here-and-now from God's fulfilment. It enables us to work thoroughly at what must be done, without anxiety over success or failure. It gives a vigilance, watch-fulness, constancy, and buoyant perseverance, but above all it is open to the Spirit, confident that the future is full of God's promise. 'We call to mind before our God and Father how your faith has shown itself in action, your love in labour, and your hope of our Lord Jesus Christ in perseverance' (St Paul, 1 *Thessalonians* 1:3).

121

Bafflement often builds up in us because we have projected outside ourselves something that is within us. The dividing line between good and evil does not lie between me and some outside system, or between myself and some 'other' group of men. It goes right through the middle of self.

Hence the primary task is to orientate our own life, to clarify issues, to be fully aware, and then to bring our own lifestyle as far as possible into line with the vision we have. It is so easy to sit in judgment on our society — to condemn its growth-materialism, its boosting of those who already have, its devouring of primary resources — and yet take no definitive steps within our own lifestyle in order to liberate ourselves from such clutter. Christ made it very clear that what blinds us from seeing things as they are is, really, sheer clutter (in his day, buying a farm or a pair of oxen, or getting married — perfectly good things in themselves, but blinding if they fill our horizon). We only have two options: if we are not part of the solution, then we must be part of the problem itself.

If we find an inner orientation to life, there comes with it a deep and inarticulate peace, the peace of knowing that the actual call given to me (that is, the precise work I am able to do) is the best thing I can do in transforming the world and giving glory to God ('the teacher must be content teaching, the administrator in administration. . . '). It is the peace of discovering in Christ not only how to transform the mess but the art of how to live in it. It is the peace of realizing that patient perseverance buoyed up by hope is the most powerful transforming force in the world.

If our own vision and orientation are right, it is amazing how many openings appear which otherwise we might never notice. The future becomes full of God's presence.

One of the deepest factors in present day bafflement is a profound sense of alienation, a sense of the whole great production line of western society rolling inevitably on quite beyond the control of any of us involved.

But the world *can* be different. Human society is not more than the people of that society. And nothing makes its 'progress' more inevitable than people who decide that it is.

It took just three years or less for Jesus to convince twelve ordinary Galileans that they were the leaven of the whole batch, the salt of the earth, the city set on the world's hill. What we need is the total conviction that things can be changed: that we can do it if we decide, in faith and hope, that it can be done. The world stands wide open — to those who decide that it does:

> 'Be at peace among yourselves.
> Warn the idlers,
> give courage to the apprehensive,
> care for the weak and be patient with everyone. .
> You must think of what is best for each other
> and for the community.
> Be happy at all times;
> pray constantly;
> and for all things give thanks to God. . .
> Never try to suppress the Spirit.'

(St Paul, 1 *Thessalonians* 5 : 14-19)

VERSES FROM PSALM 36 (37)

Do not fret because of the wicked;
do not envy those who do evil:
for they wither quickly like grass
and fade like the green of the fields.

Commit your life to the Lord and do good,
trust in him and he will act,
so that your justice breaks forth like the light,
your cause like the noon-day sun.

Be still before the Lord and wait in patience;
do not fret at the man who prospers;
a man who makes evil plots
and brings down the poor and the needy.

Calm your anger and forget your rage;
do not fret, it only leads to evil.
For those who do evil shall perish;
the patient shall inherit the land.

A little longer — the wicked shall have gone.
Look at his place he is not there.
But the humble shall own the land
and enjoy the fullness of peace.

The wicked man plots against the just
and gnashes his teeth against him;
but the Lord laughs at the wicked
for he sees that his day is at hand.

The just man's few possessions
are better than the wicked man's wealth;
for the power of the wicked shall be broken
and the Lord will support the just.

The wicked man borrows and cannot repay,
but the just man is generous and gives.
Those blessed by the Lord shall own the land,
but those he has cursed shall be destroyed.

The Lord guides the steps of a man
and makes safe the path of one he loves.
Though he stumble he shall never fall
for the Lord holds him by the hand.

Then turn away from evil and do good
and you shall have a home for ever;
for the Lord loves justice
and will never forsake his friends.